MW00584368

CONFRONTING CONFLICT

A first-aid kit for handling conflict

Friedrich Glasl

Translated by Petra Kopp

Hawthorn Press

Confronting Conflict © 1999 Friedrich Glasl
Originally published in German by Freies Geistesleben as *Selbsthilfe in Konflikten,* 1997

Published by Hawthorn Press,
Hawthorn House, 1 Lansdown Lane, Stroud, Gloucestershire, GL5 1BJ
Tel. (01453) 757040   Fax. (01453) 751138

Edited by Matthew Barton
Typeset at Hawthorn Press by Frances Fineran
Printed by The Cromwell Press, Trowbridge, Wiltshire
Cover design by Patrick Roe
Cartoons by Viv Quillan

A catalogue record of this book is available from the British Library Cataloguing in Publication Data

ISBN 1 869 890 71X

Contents

3. How can I work on myself in conflict situations?

4. How conflicts are driven

5. How conflicts can go downhill 83

6. What can I do as soon as I notice a conflict? 107

7. What can I do myself at the different levels of escalation?

8. Professional help can go further!

9. Self-knowledge and self-help in conflicts

1. Help – Conflict!

This book came about in response to numerous requests for help. As a conflict consultant I have observed a steady increase in disagreements, tensions and friction in a variety of settings and situations.

In business the pace of things has become faster and faster: products become obsolete more quickly and have to be replaced by new ones. The speed of product development means there is not enough time to test new ideas thoroughly and look at their impact, so discussion of these issues is intense, but rushed and superficial. This places many people under severe stress, which they take into their work and their families.

In politics and business new problems emerge and become intertwined: business profits and shares soar, but unemployment rises at the same time. Classic economic concepts are no longer effective in the same way as before, and this results in bitter disagreements which call traditional party political frameworks into question. This triggers confrontations between fundamentalists and realists within all parties.

Many people have come to question the conventional roles of men and women within the family and society, and as a result of various factors these roles are changing. There are winners and losers in this process, and the losers put up a fight to try to maintain old values.

Many large companies are merging with former competitors and force their staff to work with and trust their former 'enemies' immediately. In practice this leads to situations in which the differences between previous organizational cultures are emphasized, rather than the desired new common culture. This results in rivalries and exclusions.

Because of lower pupil numbers, schools now have to consider what they are about, for the first time encountering all kinds of differences between people's views of the nature of the human being, and in their practical approaches to teaching. Head teachers believe they need to impose a school philosophy in order to prevent their school stagnating in endless debates. Yet this authoritarian approach is the very reason why relationships amongst teachers, and between teachers and parents erupt into conflict.

Within the larger social context there are more and more violent clashes. So-called 'ethnic cleansing' in former Yugoslavia leads to atrocities and civil war. The tensions between Greek and Turkish Cypriots are periodically 'set alight' by politicians. In Northern Ireland there has been conflict between Protestants and Catholics for many years. Terrorist activity in Israel and Palestine, in Algeria and many other countries all over the world, only serves to make any solution of fundamental political problems seem even more remote. Anarchy, or the mafia, rule in some of the former communist countries in Eastern Europe.

In these and other such situations I have noticed that large numbers of people are helpless when it comes to conflict, and that most organizations are insufficiently equipped to handle conflict constructively. Company managers get involved in intense controversies about their strategy for the coming years – yet discussions are often suspended at the very point when real differences of opinion emerge. People don't know how to deal with this: 'It would take too long for everyone to reach agreement,' they say. As a result, those who don't support the views of the ones with power are pushed out of the organization or marginalized.

In politics, it is increasingly rare these days to see a single party with a clear majority, so there is 'horse-trading' and compromise. All this leads to a so-called 'minimum consensus', i.e. people agree to a minimum programme because there are so many reservations on all sides. Everything gets watered down to the lowest common denominator. And once the government's programme is drawn up, its implementation fails because it meets with massive resistance from those charged with putting it into practice. Each side blames the other for half-hearted measures and slow implementation. Reforms become 'stuck', thus causing more problems than they solve.

In schools people become ill and demotivated because of unresolved conflict. If difficulties are discussed in a staff meeting they often keep quiet because they don't want to get involved in more working groups, over and above their exhausting teaching work. But informal conversations tend to focus exclusively on complaints about certain colleagues who have got into difficulties with children and parents. Direct confrontations with 'problem colleagues' are avoided because everyone thinks they already have enough to worry about and deal with.

People often think that it is easier to ignore differences and swallow their anger instead of addressing issues. Often they worry that open discussion of controversies might end up destroying any goodwill that remains. Or they think, wrongly, that openly discussing differences shows lack of consideration for other people's feelings.

1.1 Conflict capability and conflict resistance

The coming decades will see great economic, political and cultural changes, and these will lead to greater problems, perhaps even violence. Because of this I am concerned that our society may develop in a fatal direction,[1] unless political and economic measures are complemented by concerted efforts to overcome our helplessness in dealing with conflict. Many experts can make a contribution in this area. However, even a whole army of professional conflict consultants or mediators would not be equal to this task. A better solution, therefore, is to help people develop their social skills so as to enable them to deal with conflict situations themselves, as far as possible. More profound conflict may ultimately require professional help, but in many cases the situation need not escalate to such an extent. This is a self-help book, intended as an aid to dealing with interpersonal tensions at work. It is a sort of 'first-aid kit' for conflict. Of course, a first-aid kit cannot replace medical advice where this becomes necessary – it may occasionally save a life, but is primarily intended to give instant help when symptoms emerge or when an accident happens.

The concepts and methods described in this book can help you to improve your conflict 'capability'. If you are involved in a conflict situation, the 'practice theories' and exercises outlined in the following chapters will help you to recognise conflict early and to fully understand the situation you are in. The concepts are like maps, helping you to find your bearings, to determine your own position on difficult terrain, as well as keeping an overview. The exercises and techniques are designed to enable you to deal with conflict in groups – at your place of work and in organizations such as councils, schools, church groups, hospitals, universities and so on. You can improve your conflict capability by carefully trying out the methods offered here.

What I mean by conflict capability is the following:
- recognizing signs of conflict in yourself and in your environment as early and as clearly as possible;
- understanding the mechanisms that intensify and entangle conflict situations;
- being able to use various methods for expressing your own position without worsening the situation substantially;
- knowing and being able to use techniques that can help to clarify positions and situations;
- recognizing the limits of your knowledge and skills; knowing when professional help is needed.

Once people become more 'conflict-capable', they can make the organizations in which they are involved more 'conflict-resistant'. I see a 'conflict-resistant' organization as being able to deal with differences, friction and tensions constructively. It is not rattled by tensions; it doesn't grind to a halt in the face of occasional resistance to taking decisions. Nowadays machines and equipment are sometimes described as being fault-resistant: shock-proof, scratch-proof, water-proof, screened against magnetic or electronic influences. If a problem does occur, this equipment is supposed to be easy to get going again. But this is exactly where many organizations have a problem: they thrive while the 'sun shines', but if it gets a little too hot, cold or wet, they have difficulties; if it gets stormy or thundery, they collapse.

1.2 Conflict avoidance versus belligerence – two extremes

There are often two very different, extremely one-sided attitudes towards conflict: individuals either *avoid conflict* or are particularly *belligerent*. Where these attitudes are shared by many people in a group, the first leads to an organizational culture in which conflict is avoided and suppressed, which in turn leads to paralysis and a loss of enjoyment, creativity and vitality; the second attitude leads to a situation in which people fight about everything and with everybody, until all common ground is destroyed (Figure 1.1).

	Conflict avoidance	**Belligerence**
Personal attitude	Retreat, escape, defensiveness; fear of disagreements; anger and emotions are suppressed; differences are hidden from the public eye	Offensive approach, aggression; enjoyment of friction; personal emotions are lived out and clearly shown; differences are fought out in public
Organizational culture	Mostly formal interaction; structures and methods encourage distance; power (attached to position, norms, methods ...) is the main emphasis	Mostly informal inter-action; structures and methods encourage con-frontation; personal power (conviction, ability, strength, emotionality ...) is played out openly
Effect in the group	'Cold conflicts'; all energy is paralysed; static and cumber-some; death through paralysis	'Hot conflicts'; hectic and overly dynamic; unsteady and super-ficial; disintegration through anarchy

Figure 1.1: Extreme personal attitudes in conflict situations and organizational cultures

Neither of these attitudes enables people to handle differences, tensions and conflict constructively. In the long term every rigidly held, one-sided attitude leads to disaster.

At a first glance this presents an insoluble dilemma. No matter which attitude you decide to take, the result seems to be negative! However, I do not look at conflict in a fatalistic way; I am only pointing out that *both attitudes are one-sided* and that something else is required. If each attitude reinforces its one-sidedness, it can lead to the downfall of a group. Whether things get that far is always determined by those involved!

This is why I place a third attitude in between the two extremes: in relation to people I advocate a 'personal conflict capability', and with regard to organizations I suggest there is a need for conflict resistance as a basic principle. First I am going to look in more detail at the two extreme personal attitudes and will point out their opposing behavioural tendencies (Figure 1.2).

Conflict avoidance		**Belligerence**
Tendency to flight: this person leaves the scene; devalues herself;[2] ranks her own interests lower than those of other people; is fearful		Tendency to aggression: this person steamrollers others; hurts and insults others; is egocentric; pursues only her own interests; is daring, arrogant

Figure 1.2: Two extreme basic attitudes towards conflict

Both attitudes are generally rooted in certain fears:[3]

- People who *avoid conflict* are afraid that they might come across as unfeeling, cold and inhuman if they behave in an aggressive manner; they worry that they might rebuff, hurt and destroy others, or that they might get hurt themselves. For this reason they avoid harsh confrontation, suppress their feelings and retreat into isolation.

- On the other hand, *belligerent people* are afraid that they might deny themselves if they are too accommodating; they hate to be considered cowardly or insecure; therefore they show their emotions, act offensively and prefer to suffer or inflict pain rather than leave the scene.

If you make yourself aware of these fears, they can't control you from your subconscious. Knowing about these fears is a prerequisite for the *third attitude, assertiveness* in conflict situations.[4] This attitude is based on the assumption that all the various people involved in a conflict situation have an equal basic right to exist and therefore the right to their own viewpoints.

Before going into these fears and ways of overcoming them, I will first discuss in more depth the *basic assumptions* behind conflict avoidance, conflict capability and belligerence (Figure 1.3).

Conflict avoidance	**Conflict capability**	*Belligerence*
Conflict drains energy, therefore: keep away from it!	**Aggressions are energy: I will channel them in positive ways!**	Conflict allows me to experience my own being – it increases my vitality!
Open conflict brings unnecessary destruction!	**Conflict helps to get away from outdated patterns!**	Only chaos will give rise to the new!
Conflict only deepens opposites; differences are basically insoluble!	**Differences are vitally necessary; working out differences benefits everyone!**	Consensus is often an illusion because: 'War is the father of all things!'

Figure 1.3: The basic assumptions behind conflict avoidance, conflict capability and belligerence

Views of the positive and negative effects of conflict, about opportunities and risks, are linked to these and other assumptions.[5] This also means that they are linked to hopes and fears.

Whether the optimistic or the pessimistic side is stronger depends on the personality and life experiences of an individual; in addition, influences from the religion, ideology, philosophy and culture of a society will also have a formative influence. The most important points about views of the benefits or disadvantages of conflicts can be summarized as shown in Figure 1.4.

In the following situation ...	*... the benefit could be:*	*... there is a danger that:*
1. There are diffuse viewpoints in the organization	At last people will take clear positions	Exaggerated and rigid stances might form
2. People don't take clear positions when there are disagreements	Individuals become clearly visible and noticeable	People show extreme and fanatical characteristics
3. Life in the group is grey and lifeless	There are intense emotions, energy is released	Emotions predominate and lead to a lack of objectivity
4. Existing structures are rigid and obstructive	Rigid forms are radically resolved	All form is destroyed, only chaos and anarchy remain
5. Old patterns of thinking are deeply embedded	Old principles and habits are questioned	Total insecurity arises, there is nothing to hold on to
6. Existing power structures suppress innovation	The balance of power changes, innovation is possible	Power and counter-power destroy one another

Figure 1.4: Views of the functions of conflicts, and of their benefits and disadvantages

Figure 1.4 shows that useful or damaging functions depend on two things: firstly on the situation a group is in before the conflict, and secondly on the degree to which an attitude is assumed to exist. It would therefore be a dangerous generalization to say that conflict always clarifies different stances or that it always strengthens a group, or whatever. In situations 1 to 3 a shapeless group would benefit from disagreement; however, if a group is already characterized by strong stances and individualism, then a disagreement will deepen these. However, if situations such as 4 to 6 occur in groups with problematic rigidities, the effects of opposition can be useful and lead to a loosening, opening and an increase in flexibility; but in extreme cases they can also lead to anarchy and power games.

Positive and negative effects arise from the tensions between two poles:

- When each of the poles operates on its own and particularly strongly, destructive imbalances arise.
- Even if a certain method had a helpful effect at first, it will create new problems if it is taken to an extreme.
- What may be a problem in one situation can offer the solution to a problem in another situation.
- Every method that is good in itself can have exaggerated and perverting effects if used excessively.

In this way exaggerating the good will lead to evil! This can be illustrated with two examples:

1) A departmental manager's concern for her staff provides support for these people and is therefore a good thing; however, if this concern is exaggerated, it becomes a way of control. If there is insufficient concern, the manager abandons her staff.

2) If an older teacher passes on her teaching experience to a younger colleague, the latter may have fewer difficulties. However, if the experienced person contributes her own wisdom at every opportunity, without being asked to do so, the young person will feel preached at and will be hindered in her development. But if there is too little help, the young teacher will feel abandoned.

1.3 Developing assertiveness

Uncovering the subconscious fears behind your basic attitudes can
help you to determine where you are coming from (Figure 1.5).

'Anne' should do this exercise together with 'Ben', a person whom
she trusts. Anne and Ben start off by using Questions 1 to 4 in
relation to Anne.

1. Consider Anne's basic attitude in relation to conflict: does she tend
towards *conflict avoidance* or towards *belligerence?* Make brief notes on
how people who know her well would describe her basic attitude:
'Anne tends to act in the following ways: ... Anne tries to avoid ...'

2. Now imagine Anne substantially intensifying her usual attitude
towards conflict:

- How would somebody who likes Anne describe the potential
  benefits of the intensification for Anne herself? 'By
  intensifying her attitude, Anne would benefit in that she ...'
- What might be the benefit of an intensification of Anne's
  previous attitude for her group? How would the group
  describe this? 'We would benefit in that ...'

3. Now imagine Anne assuming an attitude that is clearly the
opposite of her usual approach:

- Again, how would a good friend describe the disadvantages
  this might bring for Anne? 'Anne is probably worried about ...'
- How would somebody from Anne's group describe the
  potential disadvantages for the group? 'We could suffer in
  that ...'

4. Anne compares her experiences with that of her trusted partner
Ben and considers the differences between her own and other
people's views of the potential benefits and disadvantages. Anne
closely questions Ben on any aspects where his assessment of the
effects differs substantially from her own.

---

5. Now that Ben has helped Anne with Questions 1 to 4, Anne does the same for Ben. She assesses him in relation to Questions 1 to 4 and Ben does his own assessment on all the questions. The conversation again covers Steps 1 to 4.

Figure 1.5: Fears behind the basic attitudes to conflict

In order to develop *assertiveness,* I recommend that people repeatedly and critically check their own ideas about the benefits and disadvantages. In my experience most people who *avoid conflict* clearly *overestimate* the potential *disadvantages* of a more direct and openly confrontative approach, and *belligerent people* drastically *underestimate* the destructive effects of unrestrained attacks. One's own perception of the effect of basic attitudes differs greatly from other people's perceptions. When you have carried out the exercise in Figure 1.5 with a trusted partner, you should give serious attention to any substantial discrepancies in perception and use them for checking your own basic attitudes.

The next exercise, 'The art of more considerate confrontation', is intended to clarify the basis of these perceptions. To do this, Anthony needs Bridget to act as an observer and Ken to be his partner for the confrontation. It would be useful to have several more observers.

The exercise on considerate confrontation consists of three main phases:

Phase I: Killer confrontation (Steps 1–5) – Figure 1.6
Phase II: Avoidance (Steps 6–8) – Figure 1.7
Phase III: Balanced, considerate confrontation (Steps 9–11)
               – Figure 1.8

The three phases will take from 45 minutes to an hour to work through, so it is a good idea to take a break between the phases.

If this exercise is successful, Anthony will recognize to what extent his own – mostly unchecked – catastrophic fantasies prevented him from standing up for himself. In Step 5 of Phase I the positive feedback to Anthony is important. He needs to know

Phase I: Killer confrontation

1. Anthony should think of someone to whom he has long wanted to tell what he finds annoying about him, and what he thinks of him. Anthony chooses Peter, his manager. He briefly explains to Ken who Peter is and how he usually talks to him. No further information is needed.

2. Anthony prepares for his 'killer' role for a few minutes, thinking about what he wants to tell his boss, Peter. He should be as rude, inconsiderate, aggressive and insulting as possible and must not allow 'Peter' to divert him from what he wants to say.

3. Ken prepares to play the role of 'Peter' and to offer as much resistance in the confrontation as possible. Ken thinks about ways in which he could most effectively divert Anthony from the confrontation: through threats or flattery, through evasion or attack. If he knows Anthony well, he will probably have a good idea about how he can 'soften him up'.

4. Anthony conducts his killer confrontation, with 'Peter' (played by Ken) trying to divert him from the confrontation. Bridget carefully watches Anthony's behaviour. The conversation is stopped after about 10 minutes.

5. Bridget (as well as any other observers) and Ken (in the role of 'Peter') feed back their observations. Where did Anthony succeed completely, where partially? Where did he stick to his intentions? Where did Ken try to use his tactics? How did they perceive the insulting effects of Anthony's unrestrainedly aggressive behaviour? Was the extent of the damage as great as Anthony had feared? Of course Anthony also feeds back how he felt about the confrontation, which of Ken's tricks he saw through etc.

Figure 1.6: Confrontation – Phase I[6]

where he remained firm – even if he was only making inconsiderate remarks at this point. It is very important to reflect back to Anthony exactly how his behaviour affected other people: he may have thought he was using extremely hurtful and insulting language, whereas the others may have thought that he was standing up for himself for the first time.

Phase II: Avoidance

6. Bridget now prepares for a conversation with Ken (in the role of 'Peter') in which she will exaggerate somewhat Anthony's usual attitude of conflict avoidance. Bridget (as Anthony) acts this out and Ken, in the role of the boss, will be difficult and try to intensify Anthony's urge for avoidance.

7. Bridget (as Anthony) and Ken (as Peter) conduct a conversation; Anthony observes.

8. Anthony, Bridget and Ken discuss the effects of this conversation.

Figure 1.7: Considerate confrontation – Phase II[7]

In Phase II Anthony is confronted with a caricature of himself. Bridget should not hesitate to exaggerate her behaviour, but she should not become absurd. If she exaggerates too much, Anthony would not deal with this image of himself and Phase III would not achieve the desired effect.

People who avoid conflict tend to perceive the slightest signals given out by their opponent and to consider them far more important than they are meant to be. Thus they lose the energy behind their actions. They become *overly cautious,* because they continually *see an exaggerated version* of the potential negative consequences of their actions. *Belligerent people* proceed completely differently: they are *inconsiderate* because they are completely wrapped up in their actions and therefore their *ability to perceive and receive feedback* is severely restricted. They blank out their perceptions so that the opponent can't soften them up, as expressed in the phrases 'Looking neither to left nor right', and 'Being hell-bent on getting your own way'.

Phase III: Balanced, considerate confrontation

9. Finally Anthony prepares ways of conducting a conversation with Peter in which killer behaviour and avoidance behaviour are balanced.

10. Anthony conducts the conversation, with Ken ('Peter') once again trying to make things difficult; Bridget observes.

11. Afterwards the balanced, considerate confrontation is assessed: What worked? Where did tendencies towards avoidance or aggression become apparent?

Figure 1.8: Considerate confrontation – Phase III[8]

The art of 'considerate confrontation' is an important element in conflict capability. I use the term 'considerate' to mean that I don't shut my eyes and ears against my opponent, but at the same time I clearly stand up for my own viewpoint. I can show my consideration by frequently feeding back to my opponent what I have heard or seen from her.

This ability to *act and perceive at the same time* can be practised in a further exercise (Figure 1.9), which I have called 'Duet speaking'. Anthony once again needs Bridget's help for this exercise.

The aim of the exercise 'Duet speaking' is to combine standing up for a particular viewpoint with perceptiveness towards the opposing party, according to the idea of 'considerate confrontation'.

1. Anthony and Bridget agree on a straightforward current issue on which they will assume opposing viewpoints. Then they stand facing each other.

2. For the next three minutes Anthony and Bridget talk *simultaneously*. So while Bridget advances her arguments, Anthony gives his viewpoint as well.

3. Whilst Anthony and Bridget are talking, both also have to listen to the opponent's arguments; but they must never stop talking and must not allow themselves to be dissuaded from their viewpoint. At the same time they must also observe the mood, facial expression, gestures and body language of their opponent.

4. After three minutes the conversation is interrupted and both report what they heard and saw from the other person and what they understood of the content of what was said. In particular they should find out what they didn't hear or see.

5. Anthony and Bridget feed back to each other (one at a time!) how they experienced the exercise.

Figure 1.9: Duet speaking

At first glance this exercise does not appear to be aimed at considerate behaviour: initially the aim is not to allow yourself to be dissuaded from your own arguments. But as you have to open all your senses and perceive your opponent at the same time, the exercise is practice in *perceptive action*. As a next step you can practise having a controversial discussion and, while you are talking, continually confirm what arguments you heard from your opponent and what you perceived of her state of mind.

These exercises are intended to lead the one-sided basic attitudes of conflict avoidance and belligerence away from their *extreme* positions. Both attitudes contain valuable components, but these have destructive effects if they are taken to extremes. In exercises and experiments it is easier to see that the two diametrically opposed attitudes of conflict avoidance and belligerence can be reconciled in the attitudes of *assertiveness* and *considerate confrontation* in such a way that the positive elements from both extremes can be combined to beneficial effect. In this way differences can be handled creatively and constructively so that they do not turn into conflicts.

A lot has already been said about differences and conflicts, but what exactly are differences? What are social conflicts? ('Social' in this context is taken to mean conflicts between two or more people, i.e. in couples, in groups or between groups, in larger communities and large social structures. By contrast *inner conflicts* concern one individual who is at odds with herself.)

1.4 What is meant by social conflicts?

For practical and theoretical reasons I make a distinction between 'social conflicts' and 'differences'. All social conflicts are based on differences – but not all differences are automatically conflicts. Conflict only arises when further elements are added.

It's the most natural thing in the world to experience differences. It is likely that I have differences with the vast majority of humankind (Figure 1.10):

(1) we perceive most things differently; our understanding, ideas and thoughts differ fundamentally;
(2) our feelings and emotions are not the same;
(3) our wills pull us in different directions.

We experience differences with almost everybody – and on all the psychological levels shown in Figure 1.10 – (1), (2) and (3). And yet we don't live in (social) conflict with all these people. Having differences with somebody does not mean that we have a conflict with that person. Defining conflict as widely as this would be completely pointless.

In nature, moreover, differences, opposites and incompatibilities are basic prerequisites for life and development in themselves:

• A female egg and a male sperm are necessary for procreation and life.
• The tension between acids and bases is the secret of the digestive system.
• Breathing in and breathing out must alternate continuously.

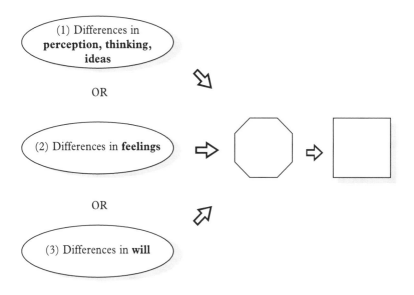

Figure 1.10: The personal factors of a social conflict:
differences on three levels[9]

- Birth and death are both necessary aspects of natural life.
- Calm and movement, sleeping and waking, summer and winter, day and night etc. are conditions of life in organic nature.
- The negative and the positive pole in magnetism and electricity, as well as gravity and levitation, are basic forces in the physical world.
- In the psychological arena, too, the polarities of joy and pain, of tension and relaxation, of sympathy and antipathy, of connecting and separating are basic facts which make feelings and emotions possible.

So the existence of differences is not the problem, as differences in themselves do not constitute conflict between people. What is important is how people handle their differences and how they experience them.

I understand a social conflict as a situation where at least one 'agent' (one party, i.e. one person, group etc.) experiences a difference in such a way that the actions of another 'agent' restrict the way in which she lives out or realizes her own ideas, feelings or intentions. As Figure 1.11 shows, actions and perceived effects are added to the differences in (1) perception, ideas and thinking – and/or the differences in (2) feelings – and/or the differences in (3) will.

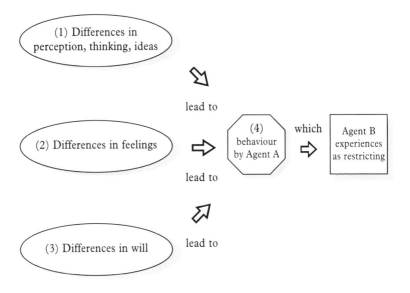

Figure 1.11: Defining elements of a social conflict[10]

It is this interaction of perceived differences in another person's behaviour (group, organization etc.), perceived as restrictive, that is meant by the definition of a social conflict:

Social conflict is an interaction
– *between agents (individuals, groups, organizations etc.),*
– *where at least one agent*
– *perceives incompatibilities between her*
      thinking/ideas/perceptions

and/or feelings
and/or will
– *and that of the other agent (or agents), and*
– *feels restricted by the other's action*[11]

For example, if the agents are two colleagues, Anthony and Ben, they don't first need to agree that they see, feel or want different things; it is enough if *at least* one of the colleagues perceives *the differences and the consequences of actions* in this way. As soon as Anthony and/or Ben perceives this, a number of elements come into play which negatively affect the interaction between the two. This is because Elements 1, 2, 3 and 4, given above to explain my definition of conflict (Figure 1.11), are the most important personal factors in every human encounter. As soon as Anthony, a teacher, thinks that his colleague Ben prevents him from realizing his ideas about modern teaching methods, there is a conflict between him and Ben. Because of this there will soon be a change in the way in which Anthony and Ben perceive each other (1), what they feel about each other (2), what they want from each other (3) and what they do to each other, by word or deed (4). In the following section I will describe only the most important changes in these factors (1) to (4).[12]

1.5 Changes in personal factors: simultaneous cause and effect

(1) Changes in perception, ideas and thinking:
In conflicts, perception is increasingly impaired, so that the people involved in the conflict arrive at different views of reality.

Different views in turn lead to more aggression; this increases the differences in perception, intensifies the anger even more and provides the stimuli for further attacks. Overall the following changes will occur in the participants – largely or completely unnoticed by them:

• Their attention becomes selective, i.e. some things are seen more clearly, others not at all.

- Threats are perceived more clearly – other things are overlooked.
- Annoying and irritating characteristics of the opponent are noticed, good traits are overlooked or belittled.
- There is an impairment of the perception of time (so-called 'cognitive short-sightedness') which means that the medium- and long-term consequences of one's own actions increasingly fade from consciousness.
- Events are perceived in a twisted, and often distorted way, so that in remembering a reversal of the chronological order can occur.
- Multifaceted and complex things or events are only perceived in a simplified way.
- People only see what they want to see, and what corresponds to their own opinion and their ingrained patterns of thinking, i.e. existing prejudices appear to be confirmed and become more rigid.

Generalizations occur in people's thinking. Polarized views and ideas arise. The problem is not only the fact that perceptions are largely falsified, muddied and distorted, but also that these images become increasingly rigid and embedded, and are difficult to change. Over time the images the opponents have created of each other increasingly come between them, *obstructing the view of the real person.*

The consequence of these insights is that you must not consider what you perceive as necessarily true. And when your opponent confronts you with stories that contradict your own perception, then usually she is not consciously lying or distorting things but subconsciously perceiving things differently – and this applies to you as well as the other! Practical help on this is given particularly in Chapter 3, and also in Chapter 7 and 8.

(2) Changes in feelings

Initially people will become more touchy, which increases insecurity and mistrust; later they will assume an armour of insensitivity. Once the disagreement has gone on for some time, the parties in the conflict can no longer bear to experience positive and negative emotions simultaneously in relation to their opponent's attitudes and actions. They reserve for themselves and their own party their positive emotions and their negative emotions for the other party; in this way the emotional situation becomes unambiguous! As the armour of insensitivity hardens, the parties in the conflict will gradually lose sympathy for each other. They increasingly lose the ability to empathize. They isolate themselves from each other emotionally and become prisoners of their own emotional state.

Any attempt to resolve conflict will aim to liberate oneself and others from the prison of one's own feelings and moods and to regain access to the other party through the ability to empathize. Chapter 6 in particular contains exercises and techniques to achieve this.

(3) Changes in will
Here, too, people become biased and paralysed. Through dis-appointments they focus on a small number of objectives, insisting on them and wanting to achieve them at any price. Their will narrows down to only a few possibilities, becoming absolute and radical. Gradually fanaticism takes hold. The longer disagreement goes on, the more subconscious, deeper layers of will are provoked: drives and instincts are awakened which were wholly natural and justified in earlier stages of personal development but which represent a retrograde step, or regression, in later developmental phases (see Chapter 9).

Conflict resolution therefore needs to contribute towards a loosening and letting go in the domain of the will. Many of the exercises and techniques contained in Chapters 3, 6, 7 and 8 seek to achieve this aim.

(4) Changes in behaviour
The changes described in (1) to (3) become mixed up and find expression in people's words and actions. Through paralysis of the will people's behaviour loses its variety, becomes poorer and simpler. The biggest problem is the fact that a coarsening in behaviour increasingly reduces the extent to which people can express their

thinking, feelings and will. What they say and do is only partly consistent with their intentions. This has many effects on other people which are not intended and mostly not even perceived in that way. This can be so pronounced that *unintentional side effects* have a stronger impact on the opponent than *intended main effects*. This leads to the emergence of dangerous *'demonized zones'* : my opponent experiences unpleasant things from me that I did not intend. She hits back and triggers things in me which she did not intend either. But both sides feel these effects, no matter whether or not they were intentional. The conflict parties blame each other – and neither side is prepared to take responsibility for the unintentional consequences. This escalates conflicts even further. Attempts to tackle conflict will examine closely the discrepancy between intentions, behaviour and effects – Chapters 7 and 8 provide some help in this.

An additional problem with all the difficulties already discussed is the fact that (1) perception/thinking/ideas, (2) feelings, (3) will and (4) actions 'infect one another' and this intensifies their negative effects. As you will only notice the annoying things about your opponent (1), you like her less and less (2) and your will hardens (3); because of this your perception (1) focuses even more on the behaviour which annoys you; you insist on taking hard measures (3) and respond with bitterness (4), and so on. After a while you have to confront the question 'Who is actually controlling this conflict?'

1.6 The core question is: 'Do I have a conflict?' – or: 'Does the conflict have me?'

This formulation is not intended as a play on words. 'The conflict has me' means that I have *lost self-control* and *self-direction*. I can consciously enter a disagreement, but at a certain level I am no longer able to keep an overview of the situation and to influence it in such a way that, by and large, only the things I intend actually occur. And *if the conflict has me* I am no longer able to step out of the situation and switch off; I am 'other-directed', i.e. controlled from the outside. My perception becomes considerably distorted; I am plagued by ideas and thoughts that I can no longer shake off; I experience emotions that can come to obsess me completely; my will is narrowed down to a small number of goals, and my behaviour becomes simpler, stereotyped and inflexible.

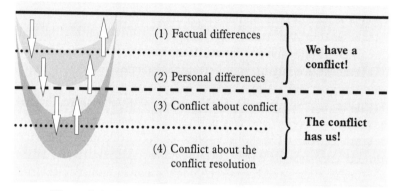

Figure 1.12: Increasing 'self-infection' in conflict situations

In conflict situations there is always a *mutual causality* or *self-infection.* In the language of systems theory this is called *circular causality.* Figure 1.12 shows how 'self-infection' can occur in the course of a difference of opinion.

Self-infection proceeds in the following way: at first there is

(1) *difference of opinion about facts.* If no agreement is reached,
(2) the *relationship* between the parties in the conflict is affected because each is annoyed about the perceived stubbornness of the other. However, the difficulties in the interpersonal relationships in turn affect the existing
(1) *factual difference,* as the opponents assume more extreme stances. This leads to an infection on the
(3) next level, to *a conflict about the conflict:* each side interprets differently the differences on the
(1) factual and (2) interpersonal levels. This increases even further the anger on
(2) the *interpersonal* level and leads to

(1) further polarization and hardening of the *factual viewpoints*. As
(3) the 'reasons and background' of the conflict are interpreted
     differently *(conflict about the conflict)*, the parties seek to resolve
     the situation in different ways, each of which is rejected by the
     other. There is now
(4) a *conflict about the conflict resolution*. All of this in turn affects
(1) the *factual differences* and
(2) the *interpersonal relationships*, and so on.
     The self-infection and intensification progress from one level to
     the next, leading to complete entanglement.

Self-help has reached its limits as soon as the infection has
advanced to level (3), as this is where the *conflict about the conflict*
begins (Figure 1.13). This applies equally to conflict amongst
conflict experts: where they have themselves become a party in the
conflict and have reached level (3), they too should seek external
professional help.
    Collegial help is not counselling by professional advisers or
consultants, but support from neutral people who are trusted by the
conflict parties.

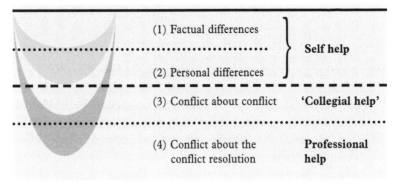

Figure 1.13: The limits of self-help in conflict situations

The limits of self-help can be explained through an analogy with the medical condition of a weakened immune system. Within certain limits the human body has its own resistance. It can deal with colds, flu and similar illnesses as long as its self-healing powers are intact. However, if the immune system itself is impaired or even destroyed by particular viruses, the body needs to be given medication. So-called 'compensatory therapy' eases the strain on the organism for a while, so that the immune system is able to return to normal. Its self-healing powers will return. However, if an organism with an impaired immune system were expected to heal itself, it would be unable to cope with this and fail.

This book seeks to show that there is great scope for self-help and support in the shape of 'collegial help'. Many techniques are intended to help people involved in a conflict to work on themselves and to take constructive action in conflict situations.

1.7 Conflict resistance of organizations

People who are conflict-capable can make a contribution in the organization where they work, so that there are opportunities for a constructive approach to differences, tensions and conflicts. In order to achieve this, certain procedures have to be established which help to recognize emerging tensions early and facilitate ways of dealing with conflict. There must also be platforms where opposites can meet and where the different ideas and interests can be dealt with. Procedures and platforms together are called *conflict regulators*[13] and are at the core of the 'conflict resistance' of an organization.

Many *procedures* can improve the conflict resistance of an organization. There are *flagging techniques* which make visible the first signs of tensions and frictions and deal with them: managers or staff from the personnel department periodically ask their colleagues where they perceive emerging problems in the working atmosphere. This questioning can be done in writing

- through *employee consultation* about the working atmosphere, about interpersonal relationships with colleagues and managers, about identification with the goals of the organization etc;

- through *complaints boxes,* with *noticeboards* in *grumble corners,* in *letters* to the in-house newsletter etc.;
- through *hot-cold maps:* the respondents anonymously colour the organizational structure red where they perceive areas of emerging hot conflict and blue in areas where 'chilly zones' are beginning to develop within the organization;
- through annual *fitness checks* (or prophylactic check-ups), in which the organization as a whole is checked for problem areas;
- through *systematic evaluation* of the available *statistics* on sickness, absenteeism, fluctuation, attrition etc.;
- through *forward-looking problem-gathering:* this is not about recording problems that are already visible today but about potential areas of tension that could arise as a result of foreseeable changes in the organization's environment (market, customers, competitors, suppliers, political changes, reorganization etc.).

Some of the written methods can be replaced by face-to-face meetings and talks, e.g.:
- *forward-looking problem-gathering* within the context of regular *departmental meetings,* or as a result of working games (simulations, roleplay, scenario planning);
- *self-diagnosis discussions* to develop particular areas;
- *feedback* amongst colleagues and between managers and their teams;
- visits by managers and their team members to other areas of the organization or to other organizations, e.g. in the context of *benchmarking activities* or as part of training activities; the visitors then feed back what they noticed in the departments they visited;
- some companies use *induction programmes* for new staff or trainees in order to gain feedback from these people after a few weeks: what did they notice about the working atmosphere? How do they perceive people's conflict capability?
- through *upward appraisal,* whereby managers are assessed by their own staff – usually in strict anonymity; if serious problems emerge, these are tackled in co-operation with qualified staff or personnel counsellors;

- through *confrontation meetings:* representatives of different departments involved in a complex work process gather information on current problems and deal with them directly or in project groups;
- *supervision* and *coaching* etc.

These are only a few possibilities. It is worthwhile checking existing procedures periodically and improving them where possible.

Once problems have been flagged up, *measures* are taken *for tackling and resolving* them: this can be done in mixed groups, or in projects etc. An important element of such measures are those that deal with *complaints management* or *grievances.*

An organization can have many platforms, roles or functions that respond to and deal with problem situations, for example:

- *peer supervision in teams* or *learning partnerships* of colleagues;
- *mentoring* systems for people who take on new responsibilities;
- *sponsors* who act as internal or external 'moral guardians' for sensitive projects, which are likely to trigger tensions and conflicts;
- *complaints committees;*
- *accident notification,* i.e. people from the personnel department or the organization's welfare team who can be approached in confidence to discuss problems experienced by individuals, in relation both to themselves and to others;
- internal and external *customer conferences;*
- joint committees and *overlapping teams* for questions that might lead to conflict;
- *ombuds functions* where people can go if they are subjected to social pressure such as *sexual harassment, racial discrimination, bullying etc.*

Such platforms and roles can create a space where people can flag up and deal with differences and conflicts. However, establishing and defining the mechanisms alone does not guarantee a constructive handling of the conflicts that are flagged up. For this to happen, conflict-capable people are needed, who, on the one hand, are not in conflict with themselves and, on the other hand, can apply practical methods to approach their opponents or partners in conflict situations.

If personal conflict capability is complemented by organizational conflict resistance, an organization can confidently face the challenges which coming years will bring.

2. Personality as a source of social conflict

2.1 The threefold core of human personality

Conflicts affect our whole personality. The more a conflict escalates, i.e. the more we become entangled in it, the more it threatens to corrupt all our thoughts, feelings and will and to dominate our actions. In disagreements with our opponent we can be overcome by profound doubts about the issues in the conflict, about the purpose of the disagreement and about ourselves.

Therefore conflict, over time, always confronts us with existential decisions: are we adhering to certain norms and values that we have held dear, or are we sacrificing them in order to assert ourselves physically or psychologically? Conflict can become a question about life itself, in material, psychological and spiritual terms. Therefore existential questions demand a real answer. This chapter offers help with this.

Theoretical and practical work with social conflict leads to a deeper examination of human personality. Looking at the internal and external conflicts of his patients, Sigmund Freud developed his theory of the three psychological levels of human personality, whereby 'Id', 'Super-Ego' and 'Ego' interact with a great deal of tension. Later conflict psychologists describe different levels or components of human personality, between which there can be tension or harmony.

My own theoretical work on conflict, as well as my practical work as a consultant, is based on a view of the human personality in terms of a trinity of body, soul and spirit:[1]

- a person's *body* enables him to take part in the physical world and the forces of nature;
- with the *soul* he lives in his own inner world and in the social world, is influenced by others and in turn influences them;

- as a *spiritual being* a person takes part in spiritual realities, in the form of values and ideals.[2]

I agree with the Viennese psychiatrist Viktor Frankl[3] that we can only understand human and social events if we do not reduce people to their physicality or to merely psychological-material elements. Body, soul and spirit are the three dimensions of the holistic, indivisible human being.

The manifestation of the *spirit* in people is the human *Ego*. However, my Ego is not a finished entity: it develops throughout my life. One side of the Ego can be guided and inspired by 'Light', expressed by values and ideals; the other side must also confront the 'Shadow', the carnal nature of my being, with my insufficiencies, imperfections and weaknesses. So in everything I do and don't do, my Everyday Ego finds itself in this tension between Light and Shadow. My Ego constantly lives in this tension and can develop through it – or can fail because of it.

In the same way the core of human personality is understood to be threefold, as shown in Figure 2.1. We all want to 'make something of ourselves' and strive to make the most of our abilities because we carry inside us an image of a 'better person'. For all of us this image is individually, exclusively and uniquely shaped by ourselves.

I can list a number of positive characteristics, aspirations and goals and will recognize that these are a coherent whole, that is, they show a certain consistency, a certain configuration. They exist within me not as an accidental and careless mixture; they form a certain inner 'being'. I can consider them in combination as the 'Light' image of my personality, in the sense that 'this is what I want to become, this is how I see the ideal me'. Even in childhood we get occasional glimpses of the potential personality we aspire to. Many children experience this particularly strongly around the age of nine.[4] At around 18 or 19 this orientation appears as the ideal and idol to young people, as a dream of meaningful and successful life; around age 24 it will mostly surface once again, as the vision of one's own mission – this time in a more earthly manner as a professional or life goal. With each crisis in later life the images of

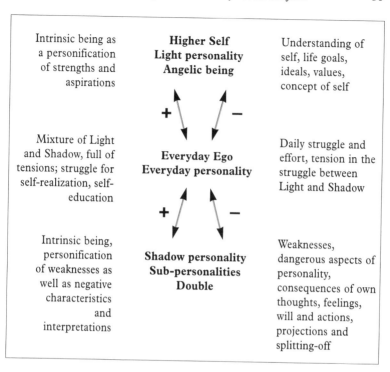

Figure 2.1: The threefold core of human personality

our yearnings and ideals will reappear.[5] Taken together, they are the image of my 'Higher Self', my 'Light', my 'angelic being', which guide my inner being.

In every human being the luminous image is in contrast with another, which takes the shape of his negative characteristics, weaknesses and immoral aspirations and desires. This, too, has a certain characteristic wholeness for each person and represents a quasi-person, the 'Shadow personality',[6] the personal 'Double'. On the basis of anthroposophy Bernard Lievegoed[7] showed how being confronted with our own 'Double' can become an incisive experience for all of us during the course of certain profound life crises.

For me the *Higher Self* is not only a 'hypothetical description' of a part of our personality, but has a real quality of existence; it takes the character of a being. As my 'angelic being' it has an inspirational, guiding or accompanying function. My Everyday Ego, that is, my immature Ego, tries to get in touch with the being of my Higher Self and to enter into a dialogue with it. In daily life and in my interaction with the real social environment, it represents the connection to the Higher Self.

The Double or *Shadow* is not merely an auxiliary label either; it is an intrinsic being which I myself have created over the course of my life, through all the things I have done and not done. It is only in the last hundred years that the phenomenon of the Double has been investigated scientifically, although it appears in literature much earlier. A.-M. Rocheblave-Spenlé[8] shows that this experience was first seized on in philosophy (for instance in Pascal's ideas about 'man's dual nature between angel and devil'), then in literature (Corneille, Goethe, Pirandello, Wilde, Dürrenmatt and others). At times my fellow human beings can see the essence of my Double more directly and clearly than I myself can. Then they will reflect back to me this reality of my being – often full of bitterness and reproaches. But because as yet I myself do not have such a clear image of my Double, I vehemently reject such 'feedback' as unjustified, even insulting incriminations.

In general we are only able to directly experience these sides of our being in a small number of, often very dramatic, moments of our life. Humanistic psychology[9] calls these 'peak experiences'. I remember episodes in my life where I had been deeply humiliated by others; suddenly the figure of my Double stood in front of me – inescapable, even extremely menacing. And I was overcome by the feeling that the people around me did not recognize the whole of my being but were reducing and fixating me only to my Shadow: 'This is how you are! Don't try to get out of it – just admit that you are evil through and through!' In such moments of deepest shock there is a danger that we actually allow ourselves to be wholly identified with our Double. Wilhelm Busch once put it in these lighthearted words: 'Once your reputation is in ruin, it doesn't matter what you're doing'. This can go so far that people forfeit contact with their Higher Selves and completely surrender to the powers of their Doubles.

However, we all also know what it is to be imbued, at certain moments, with our Higher Self. Particularly at times of profound shock people can directly experience the conviction that, next to their clearly visible Shadow personality, there is also a Light-filled personality, which accompanies them as long as they don't break off the contact. During moments of extreme spiritual/psychological or physical exertion, perhaps also after a particular achievement at work, in the creative field or in sports, we can have strong experiences of our angelic being.

In my life these encounters were at their most intense when I was able to support my wife and actively help during the birth of our three children. Faced with a newly born human being helplessly entrusting himself to the care of his parents, the soul is suddenly confronted with the overwhelmingly joyous, luminous image of one's own Higher Self. I remember similar moments on occasions of extreme danger, e.g. when, as a student, I was responsible for a group of students from different countries undertaking a risky tour in high mountains. In critical moments a visionary clarity suddenly showed me what I had taken on in my life.

We also know the happy experience of doing something for somebody else that inspires hope, warmth and confidence in that person. On such occasions the almost 'tangible' proximity of our Higher Self is a fact of experience that even sceptics can't argue away.

2.2 The connections between the Everyday Ego and the Higher Self

My Everyday Ego can connect with the Higher Self or with the Shadow in very different ways. The nature of these inner connections determines whether there are tensions, friction and conflict in my external interaction with other people. The different connections between the Everyday Ego and the Higher Self, and between the Everyday Ego and the Double, adopt typical forms which can be characterized – whereby the most frequent forms are located between two extreme poles (Figure 2.2).

The connection between the Everyday Ego and its Light and Shadow can be characterized either by great proximity or by great distance. If *proximity/nearness (N)* dominates, the Everyday Ego can completely identify with one or the other aspect of its intrinsic being. If *distance (D)* dominates, this can lead to the view that one has nothing to do with the other aspect and is not responsible for its influence. The first connection creates an illusion of identification, the other of illusory repression and splitting-off. The Everyday Ego can no longer recognize and accept certain aspects of its personality as its own and it therefore projects negative characteristics onto others.

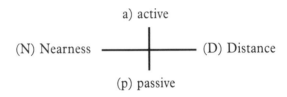

Figure 2.2: Basic attitude between two extreme polarities

If the active side (a) predominates, the individual will tend to deal with the other aspect of its being. But when the passive attitude (p) dominates, then the individual more or less surrenders to the powers of the Shadow or the Light.

I will now describe four basic attitudes, where a connection between the two polarities can be shown (Figure 2.3). They are presented in the form of a conversation, as if the Everyday Ego were having a dialogue with the Higher Self. This might help you to recognize which basic attitude you tend towards on different occasions.

(1) Compulsive self-chastisement

You seem so big and powerful! And I am so small and weak in comparison with you. But I do not want to let go of you, my higher being. If necessary I will force you to connect with me. I want to become like you. I want to be ruthless with myself and do everything to be like you! The people around me will have to recognize that I am doing everything in my powers to become like you. They will have to acknowledge my

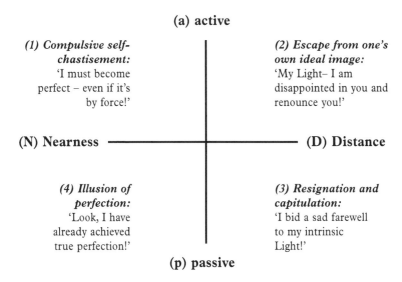

(a) active

(1) Compulsive self-chastisement:
'I must become perfect – even if it's by force!'

(2) Escape from one's own ideal image:
'My Light– I am disappointed in you and renounce you!'

(N) Nearness ———————— **(D) Distance**

(4) Illusion of perfection:
'Look, I have already achieved true perfection!'

(3) Resignation and capitulation:
'I bid a sad farewell to my intrinsic Light!'

(p) passive

Figure 2.3: Problematic basic attitudes of the Everyday Ego in relation to the Higher Self

positive efforts and judge me accordingly! Therefore I will be relentlessly strict with myself and force myself to realize my Higher Self! I will inexorably purge myself of everything that stands in my way!

In my work I have come across a manager who lived this attitude and who imposed great duties and the strictest demands on himself. This man was often unbearable to the people around him. He could not see his own weaknesses, did not want to see that he in no way corresponded to the ideal image he had of himself – however hard he tried! In addition he closed himself off from any criticism from others. His secretary complained that her boss could not accept that he himself occasionally made mistakes. Instead he claimed that the mistakes were the secretary's fault; after all, a man of his stature, somebody who had such high goals in the important aspects of his job, could not be identified with everyday human weaknesses in such trifling matters!

In this attitude there is a strong connection between the active pole (a) and nearness (N). There is great effort to achieve a merging with the Higher Self, even if the environment recognizes that this is an illusion and suffers as a result.

(2) Escape from one's own ideal image

Yes, you are great! You ask a lot of me – and I am not worthy of you. In fact, I am frightened of you. I see you as admonishing me, but I cannot live up to your expectations. Your pure light hurts my eyes. I must close my eyes so that you do not blind me. I will avoid you so that my insufficiencies do not constantly depress me, perhaps even destroy me.

I once knew a teacher who tried hard in his work to interact patiently and lovingly with his pupils. But at home, with his own children, he could not do this. He knew that, as a father, he did not live up to his educational ideals and thus undermined his credibility. Therefore his domestic situation became unbearable for him. He escaped into many unimportant activities, where he advanced his educational ideas but through which he also escaped from family life.

This attitude is very close to the poles of distance (D) and active (a).

(3) Resignation and capitulation

O higher being – you are so beautiful, perfect and great! I will never come close to your perfection. Compared to you I am only small and unimportant. I will never become as great and beautiful as you. I sadly bid you farewell.

In this attitude the Everyday Ego has distanced itself (D) from its higher ideals and has resigned (p) and retreated. Sometimes the memory of these – too highly pitched – ideals is still cherished in various forms of 'Sunday Christianity'. We know plenty of people in our life (perhaps you and I belong to this group?) who forget their ideals in the harsh realities of their professional life. They can only hark back sentimentally to their ideals, 'for which unfortunately the world is too rotten', in quiet moments of contemplation, on vacation or on holiday.

(4) Illusion of perfection

How far have I come! My high goals and ideals – I am living them already. I am my Higher Self. Other people must recognize that I have reached a high level of development and purity. They must recognize and revere their great, luminous example in me!

In my work I once encountered the prior of a monastery; he was feared and avoided by his monks, who saw him as arrogant and unapproachable, even deeply inhuman. He believed, they felt, that he practised the ideals of the order's founder to such an extent that he was already a saint. His fellow monks, on the other hand, saw his many weaknesses all the more sharply and suffered as a result. Thus passivity (p) dominated in the shape of self-righteousness – 'Perfection has been attained!' – and very close proximity (N), illusory identification.

These four basic attitudes of the Everyday Ego to the Higher Self are the most common in daily life. It is easy to see that in each of these attitudes the approach to dealing with one's own ideals – that is, with the image we have formed of ourselves – is very problematic and must lead to internal as well as external tensions and conflicts.

2.3 Problematic connections between the Everyday Ego and the Double

The most important basic attitudes towards one's own Shadow, the Double, can be described in a similar way (Figure 2.4). They are again illustrated in a conversation between the Everyday Ego and the unfriendly aspect of our personality, the Double.

These attitudes are described in the following sections.

(1) The determined lion tamer

O Shadow, you are so mighty! You threaten to overcome me. Therefore I will guard myself against you. As soon as I notice the slightest sign of your activities within me, I will attack you, fight you, overcome you and bind you! Then I will dominate you and tame you. I will let you feel my anger at the slightest resistance.

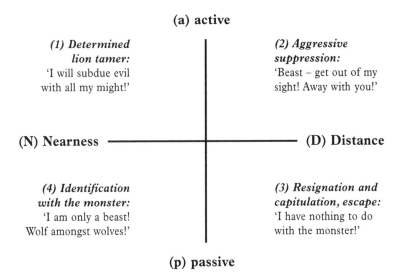

(a) active

**(1) Determined
lion tamer:**
'I will subdue evil
with all my might!'

**(2) Aggressive
suppression:**
'Beast – get out of my
sight! Away with you!'

(N) Nearness ———————————— **(D) Distance**

**(4) Identification
with the monster:**
'I am only a beast!
Wolf amongst wolves!'

**(3) Resignation and
capitulation, escape:**
'I have nothing to do
with the monster!'

(p) passive

*Figure 2.4: The problematic basic attitudes of the
Everyday Ego in relation to the Shadow*

I once worked with a very respected scientist, who had become the head of a research department. With his attitude of 'no-compromise-science', which had helped him to succeed in his scientific research, he quickly foundered as a manager. He then reproached himself fiercely; he could never forgive himself for his own weaknesses but chastised himself mercilessly for his mistakes. This rigid attitude was very difficult for his colleagues as it overshadowed all the positive elements in their boss's character as well as his self-respect.

In this attitude nearness (N) and activity (a) dominate.

(2) Aggressive suppression
Dark Shadow, you are a dangerous beast. I don't know how you got into my house. You must have come from others, somebody must have brought you into my house. You are a complete stranger to me. I hate you and cannot tolerate the sight of you! When I have visitors in the house, I will lock you up in the cellar. Get away! I don't want to hear or see you!

I saw this attitude most clearly in a therapist, who repeatedly provoked anger and resistance in his patients because he often made mistakes with appointments that had been arranged; he was frequently late, forgot the diagnosis he had made etc., but he would not admit this. Yet he fiercely criticized the same shortcomings in his patients. He aggressively fought these 'dangerous' mistakes and 'pathological patterns of behaviour' in them – as a substitute for tackling these problems in himself.

This attitude is often characterized by covert self-hatred. It is dominated by activity (a) and distance (D).

(3) Resignation and capitulation, escape

Shadow, you are much stronger than I! I have often tried to fight or tame you, but you follow me wherever I go! Now I have given up fighting you. I am tired of it. Leave me in peace! In future I will go out of my way to avoid you.

The presence of the Shadow is passively tolerated; responsibility for one's own deeds is rejected. Passivity (p) and distance (D) dominate.

A senior civil servant had been attacked from all sides because of his shortcomings in his interactions with staff, colleagues and politicians. Every time he was criticized, he pointed out, with an air of innocence, many structural, political and legislative weaknesses as well as financial constraints and his own powerlessness in the face of these restrictions. So when there were problems, they were rarely down to him, always down to external factors beyond his control. Even when his attention was drawn directly to personal weaknesses, he shrugged these off: 'It's the system that's wrong; no human being is perfect. Look at the other departments: they are managed in the same way as I manage here! And besides: people of my age can no longer change.'

(4) Identification with the monster

Yes, monstrous Shadow, you are here! And I recognize that basically I am only a beast! You are my true self. There is no point in denying you. Well, I will acknowledge the beast within me and behave like a beast. After all, this is how I am – and all others are the same!

Here the experience of one's Shadow is so overwhelming that any connection with the Higher Self is denied. The dominating poles are nearness (N) – identification – and passivity (p) – complete surrender to the powers of the Double.

All four problematic basic attitudes of the Everyday Ego towards the Shadow, or Double, are shown in Figure 2.4 in relation to the polarities given. In all these cases an individual's strength is wasted in a fruitless connection with his own Shadow.

2.4 The inner tension is projected outwards

In all of the eight basic attitudes described the Everyday Ego lives in tension with the Higher Self or the Double. The Ego can't cope with the challenges and therefore seeks a way out that promises a reduction in the inner tensions it experiences – even if this escape is superficial or short-term.

However, the eight problematic attitudes in relation to one's own Light and Shadow, described above, can be contrasted with positive and constructive basic attitudes which I call the 'attitude of self-confrontation' (Section 2.6). With these attitudes people can try to face the challenges of the Light and Shadow and to work actively to overcome tensions. Before going into this, however, I will mention the example of five typical forms of interpersonal conflict, examined and described by Horst-Eberhard Richter.[10] Where the Everyday Ego is unable to deal constructively with the two other sides (Higher Self and Double), inner tensions can easily be shifted, or exported, to the outside. This leads to typical conflicts in the interpersonal area.

Most people see tensions and conflicts as they would see accidents: they are not their fault, and they reject them. Ultimately they don't take full responsibility for their own behaviour in threatening and unpleasant situations. They could, however, also try to address the challenge presented by crises or tensions, as these situations make a particularly powerful call on our Higher Self. At the same time, though, they also provoke our Double. The decisive factor is whether or not I respond by thinking something along the lines of: 'Who cares?! I'm being attacked – so I will prove that I cannot be steamrollered easily! I will resist and show my strength. Toughness and intransigence are justified in a situation like this!'

In tense situations, when we are provoked, it is all too easy *not* to act on the basis of our better moral qualities. Instead the 'animals' of the Double in us are provoked; gradually these will begin to fight back and their actions will become mixed up with our behaviour. Indignation and anger can overcome us until – more or less in blind anger and without thinking – we hit back. This involves hurtful words or even physical force. In this situation our Double has kept the upper hand. For reasons of security and self-assertion we often resort to old ways of behaviour which we had already renounced. Reverting to a pattern of behaviour that we have already recognized as unethical and overcome (regression) can be clearly recognized in the eight basic attitudes described above and in the five forms of conflict which follow.[11]

These situations see the occurrence of social-psychological mechanisms of 'projection' that are typical for social conflict.[12] One conflict party sees in the opposing party exactly those weaknesses which – if it had sufficient self-knowledge! – it should reproach itself for.[13] But in order to justify its own actions, each conflict party creates a flattering image of its own personality. Each side sees itself as more intelligent, morally superior, more courageous than the other,[14] and blames the other, even 'demonizing' it as the conflict intensifies.[15]

The images of the conflict parties that have emerged in this way are no longer identical with the normal image of the Higher Self and the Shadow; they are exaggerations and distortions. The dynamics of the conflict cause the parties to exaggerate these images. Once the self-image and the enemy image have moved apart to such an extent, it seems justifiable to condemn the opposing party as 'evil through and through'. What is tragic is the fact that in conflict situations these exaggerations and distortions occur unintentionally and subconsciously. As the opponents no longer interact openly and directly, their perception is restricted. Therefore they cannot recognize possible distortions for what they are and remove them. In a conflict situation the 'filtering of perception'[16] leads to an intensification of previously held prejudices. It would be right to say that in a fierce conflict the opponents no longer fight each other directly. Instead, the image I have built up about myself fights the image that I have built up of my enemy and on which I am more or less fixated. We could say that on the one hand conflict *over*-sensitizes us towards the Shadow aspects of our opponent, and on the other hand it closes us off against pointers to our own Shadow sides, whereby we feed illusions about our Higher Self.

2.5 Some basic forms of interpersonal conflict

Based on a fairly similar view of human personality, the psychiatrist Horst-Eberhard Richter[17] has, in the context of family therapy, examined different conflict relationships between parents and children, and has formulated types of role assignments that hold a lot of conflict. However, such disturbed relationships are not only found between parents and children. In my work on conflict within companies, hospitals, schools and public offices I have found corresponding relationships outside of the family unit. The most important of these basic forms are now described.

(1) 'I am your judge!'
If someone feels unable to satisfy the demands of their own Higher Self, they may compensate by continually judging and criticizing others and trying to get them to meet these demands in their lives. Through this they lose their spiritual and psychological freedom, not really living their own lives but that of others. The active (a) and distance (D) poles predominate.

I once had to deal with a fierce conflict in a council office. A senior council officer, aged around 60, was embroiled in confrontation with a 40-year-old councillor, his most senior political superior. Both belonged to the same political party. The 60-year-old council officer had also been working as a part-time lecturer, training party officers for many years, and some time ago had also trained his current boss, the younger councillor. Following initial discussions and debate the older man took on the role of 'conscience' for the younger, successful politician. Every public speech by the politician was sharply criticized by his former teacher whenever the latter thought that it contained something 'ideologically impure'. As an ideological mentor the older man demanded constant exemplary behaviour from his former pupil. The relationship between the two became increasingly difficult. Over time the politician felt as if he was being persecuted by his 'judge'. A characteristic of this conflict was the fact that the older man continually wanted to set the norms and values the younger politician had to live up to. So the latter had to live his ideological mentor's ideals – which the mentor had projected from his own Higher Self onto his pupil because he himself was unable to have a political career. In this conflict the politician fought against such moral persecution.

(2) 'You are the better part of me!'
This conflict, too, arises from an inability to meet the demands of one's own Higher Self. The poles passive (p) and distance (D) dominate.

I once encountered a drastic example of the sorts of conflict that this attitude can give rise to. An adult education teacher had high ideals, but she felt too weak as an individual to realize these, and therefore joined an existing group. In her imagination and expectations she quickly came to idealize and idolize this group: 'On my own I am too weak, but as a group we can complement and help one another! We will show the educational community what good adult education could look like.' The expectation of the group was that it was better at doing things than each member on his own. After a short time there were disappointments, which gradually grew into severe frustrations: team work made everything a little more complicated, difficult and slow. No clear decisions could be reached, nobody felt responsible for their practical implementation, etc. The teacher then heaped bitter reproaches on the group because she had 'expected something completely different from this particular team' and she now felt betrayed. Initially the individual members of the group had – without noticing – idealized and idolized one another. The potential of the collective had become highly idealized. Over time this turned into 'negative idolization',[18] which ended in collective feelings of guilt after the group had dissolved.

(3) 'You are the weaker part of me'

H-E. Richter[19] describes how many families do something like keeping a 'family fool': one of the children becomes the clown and keeps making the silliest remarks, behaves clumsily and helplessly. The others both laugh about and pity him at the same time. A role is therefore created in which this person always has to take on the weaknesses of the family, whilst the other brothers and sisters and the parents see themselves as skilful, intelligent, successful etc. This (more or less subconscious) role assignment enables the other members of the family to appear better people, as all the weaker characteristics keep being focused and projected onto the scapegoat. Often children fight against this imposed role for many years once they have realized that they have been manoeuvred into it against their will. These conflicts are based on one-sided projection of aspects of the Double onto another person, with the passive (p) and distance (D) poles dominating.

Similar situations can arise in a work context, for example when a production department keeps blaming the planners or designers for mistakes, or if management holds the 'stupid, work-shy frontline staff' responsible for every mistake. This is a way of avoiding the need to look for mistakes in one's own behaviour. So projection often serves to offload guilt onto other people. At times of high unemployment there is often great competition in the workplace, with bullying or 'mobbing' [20] aimed at hounding people out of their job. Mobbing often operates on the dynamics described above.

(4) 'You are the dangerous aspect of my being'

In small families, in groups and in larger organizations there is often a tendency to look for scapegoats who can be blamed for dangerous developments or who, as competitors for jobs, can simply be pushed out through 'mobbing'. In the wider context of society this leads to attacks on certain minority groups which are then persecuted and – as in the case of anti-Semitism – ruthlessly purged. The attacked and persecuted group is generally assigned all those characteristics which are the opposite of the – assumed – virtues of the powerful group. So, for example, if a group sees itself as courageous, intelligent, clean, honest and creative, the scapegoat opponent must automatically be cowardly, dirty and smelly, dishonest and culturally destructive. This is the nature of religious and ethnic prejudices, wherever these occur throughout the world. So the opponent is seen only as a Shadow, and becomes the target for projecting characteristics that one sees as most negative in oneself – even though their very existence in oneself is denied.[21]

In the scapegoat mechanism the sum total of all positive characteristics and moral qualities is reserved for oneself, resulting in a manic distortion of one's own Higher Self, while the opponent is wholly identified with the Double. Such extreme forms develop only during the escalation of a conflict (Chapters 4 and 5) and culminate in the fifth level of escalation. At the beginning of the escalation the two sides may have had only a slight feeling of superiority, but through actions and counteractions this can gradually turn into a complete rejection of the opponent.

In this situation the active (a) and distance (D) poles dominate.

(5) 'Just be normal – like I am!'

Some people have learned from many conflicts to cut themselves off from their Higher Self and from their Shadow. They dismiss all 'talk about ideals and so on' as 'sheer nonsense', as 'opium for the people'. But they also reject responsibility for the Shadow aspects of their thinking, feelings and will, 'because people aren't angels, after all!'.

This dynamic is characterized by the attitudes passive (p) and distance (D). For example, a father and his two sons had been arguing for many years. The key to understanding the father and his behaviour lay in his life story: as a teenager he had allowed himself to be blinded and seduced by Hitler's ideology. When he was 17 his idealistic aspirations led him to sign up voluntarily for military service and during the last months of the war he fought at the front.

He wasn't released from Russian imprisonment until about ten years after the end of the war. Later he encountered hostility in his hometown because of his youthful fanaticism and was held partly responsible for many excesses of the Hitler regime. He recognized that he had allowed himself to be led astray in his search for ideals. So he decided to make a radical break with all ideals and ideologies; but he categorically rejected any share of responsibility for the atrocities of the Nazi regime. Over time he also denied any responsibility for weaknesses or mistakes he might have himself. For him, being 'normal' meant recognizing neither his Higher Self nor his Shadow. His two sons had to behave accordingly, although they themselves were searching for ideals and inspiring values – e.g. in the scout movement. Their father used every opportunity to label these ideals as illusory, to mock them and to attack them. He thought his sons would be better off becoming sober businessmen.

2.6 The positive attitudes of self-confrontation and self-development

So far I have shown how we can reach a better understanding of different conflicts within ourselves and in our environment by distinguishing an Everyday Ego, a Higher Self and a Double. However, the eight problematic attitudes described are not the only imaginable attitudes. There are constructive attitudes too.

It is possible to achieve a relationship both to the Higher Self and the Double without either demanding an impossible, radical moral transformation from one day to the next or despondently throwing in the towel after repeatedly making mistakes.

The constructive basic attitudes of self-confrontation and self-development are best illustrated in the form of a conversation, as before.

The Everyday Ego could also say to the Higher Self: *Here I am with all my shortcomings and with all my good intentions. Here you are, my Higher Self, as a reminder and a challenge. Even if I have occasionally forgotten or betrayed you, you have still guided me subconsciously. I want to open myself to you. Through small steps and constantly practising I can give you space in my thinking, feelings and will and in my daily actions. Even if I can't change completely from one day to the next, I will still be content to get closer to you each day, little by little!*

And my Everyday Ego could say to my Double: *You are the Shadow of my personality. I know that the mistakes in my thinking, feelings and will and the shortcomings in my actions have created you. Therefore I am responsible for you and the effects you have. But you are not my true ego, you are just one aspect of my being. Through you I have created for myself a constant challenge. In many encounters with other people you show yourself as you really are. Therefore I do not want to react with hurt and rejection when other people point out some of your traits. Instead I want to examine their signals self-critically and to accept them as a challenge. It is not my task to suppress you by force, or to get rid of you, or to transform you from one day to the next, but to change you, patiently and constantly, through small actions. By working on myself consistently, I can transform you through my deeds and can release you from your ugly shape – which carries my own traits after all.*

The eight basic attitudes described (Figure 2.3 and 2.4) have shown what can happen if it is not possible to create a constructive balance between the active and the passive side, and between distance and nearness. This failure then leads to a reversal of the qualities of the poles 'nearness–distance' and 'active–passive', as shown in the following paragraph.

If we do not succeed in creating a self-critical distance from our own actions and omissions, we offload our unwanted mistakes and weaknesses onto our environment. That is, we *distance* ourselves in a pathological way from the unpleasant aspects of our personality and project them onto other people. At the same time we take the credit for the positive effects of the actions of other people, aspiring towards *nearness* and identification. The active and passive poles, too, are perverted through the eight problematic basic attitudes: in one case there is passive 'tolerance' towards one's own shortcomings, whilst the same characteristics are fiercely fought in other people. So the action of change is not aimed at one's own inner life but at changing the external environment. The attitude of self-confrontation, on the other hand, leads me to work hard on myself and thus transform my relationships with other people. This creates the most important basis for *actively and constructively dealing with conflict.* The prerequisite for the basic attitude of self-confrontation and self-development can be shown schematically as in Figure 2.5.

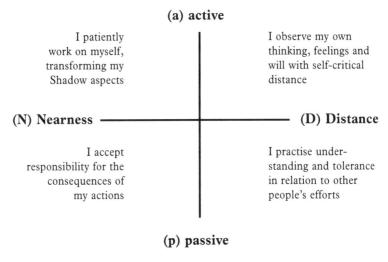

(a) active

| I patiently work on myself, transforming my Shadow aspects | I observe my own thinking, feelings and will with self-critical distance |

(N) Nearness ──────────────┼────────────── (D) Distance

| I accept responsibility for the consequences of my actions | I practise under-standing and tolerance in relation to other people's efforts |

(p) passive

Releasing the enemy within – through understanding!
Presenting to the enemy the gift of resurrection – through forgiveness!

Figure 2.5: Transforming the four polarities through the attitude of positive self-confrontation and self-development

Whereas before I *one-sidedly applied one force only to the external world,* I now apply it to myself, in order *to work more strongly on my inner life.* The quality of *nearness* and *passivity* thus becomes a readiness to take responsibility: I want to take on the consequences of my actions – even if they are unintentional and subconscious side effects! To do this I have to face other people without rejection. If I plan to work on myself – even if I have to put up with repeated setbacks – I will develop the quality of *nearness* and *activity* in the right way.

Linking the qualities *active* and *distance* becomes the ability to observe and recognize one's own thinking, feelings and will with self-critical distance, without immediately falling prey to justification, reinterpretation or projection. The qualities of *distance* and *passivity* become understanding and tolerance towards the – often equally unsuccessful – efforts of other people to overcome their weaknesses and to realize their Higher Selves in daily actions.

2.7 Light and Shadow in the identities of groups and organizations

So far I have described problems that can occur between two individuals and can lead to conflict-laden interactions between them. But everything that has been described so far can also occur in groups and organizations, and between groups. This is because a group, an informal community or a formal organization also has an identity that lives in the tension between Light and Shadow, like the Everyday Ego of an individual.

If people unite behind an idea, because they want to set up a club, a company, an action group or similar, they are brought together by their hopes.

In their first encounters they will be fascinated by all those things which they perceive as aspects of the Light in one another. In their search for common ideals, values and goals they will initially pay attention only to the things which confirm their positive expectations. It is this enthusiasm for a common project which gives them the stimulus required for pioneering initiatives.[22] It is easy to lose sight of the less positive – but nevertheless real – characteristics of their fellow founders. People idealize one another to a greater or lesser extent, which leads to a climate of 'positive idolization'.[23] But over time people will also have less positive experiences with one another. They will notice the odd weakness in their colleagues. When the disappointments accumulate and people are insufficiently self-critical, the 'positive idolization' can suddenly turn into 'negative idolization'[24] if people consider the realization of their ideals to be in danger. Then they will predominantly perceive the Shadow sides of other people and all the mechanisms described above can occur.

Groups which aspire towards high ideals are particularly susceptible to crash from positive into negative idolization: these could be organizations based on religion or ideology; political and citizens' action groups; ecologically orientated protest movements; alternative schools with an explicit educational philosophy; companies with alternative product ideas and new ways of working.

However, I want to caution against one false conclusion: conflict does not arise from people aspiring towards high ideals *per se*. Failure, rather, is caused by shortcomings of organizational structure. This is because in the phase of positive idolization the possibility of conflict is generally overlooked. Therefore methods and bodies that can be called on when tensions and disappointments emerge are not created in advance. This is the typical 'honeymoon' illusion. What is important is that people are conflict-capable and organizations become conflict-resistant, as described in Chapter 1. They are then better able to deal with high expectations as well as with contradictions and failure.

At present many organizations describe their ideal image of themselves in the form of a vision, a 'mission statement', a guiding image, or similar. In such a self-image a group describes how it wishes to be seen, in which direction it wants to develop and what it aspires to. If a group jointly develops a vision, this can contribute a great deal to the clarification of its expectations and can prevent conflict.

A guiding image, a mission or a vision is a description of the Light, or the Higher Self, of an organization. But the Shadow also becomes visible when a vision is developed: discrepancies between ideals and reality emerge. Therefore it is advisable to describe the Shadow of the group as well. The next chapter shows what you can do to put the theory into practice.

3. How can I work on myself in conflict situations?

All of the following exercises are based on the positive attitude of self-confrontation and self-development as described in Chapter 2. If, as a conflict party, you seriously apply Methods 1 to 6 to yourself, you will probably be able to meet your opponent differently from before. To do this you do not need to come to an agreement with your opponent, but you can work on yourself exclusively. However, it is advisable to ask a person whom you trust to support you in the exercises.

The exercises in Figures 3.8 to 3.13 can also be used in groups without a facilitator, in order to work on the tension between the Light and Shadow of the group's identity. Of course it would be even better to enlist 'collegial help' or the support of a professional; but the chances of success are good even without external help.

3.1 How can I work on problematic one-to-one relationships?

The methods described in Chapters 3, 6 and 7 are designed for working through certain question with the opposing party, without recourse to external professional help. However, this presupposes two things:
1. that there is at least fundamental consensus that the conflict is to be tackled, and
2. that the escalation has not yet crossed the threshold to level 4, described in Chapter 5.

However, even if the conflict has escalated further, you can still benefit from working through Methods 1 to 6. They make it possible for you to really let go of the other conflict party once you have said good-bye to them. These methods have often been used successfully to clarify and tackle difficulties in one-to-one relationships. Through them you should be able to release blockages and fixations and thus to release the enemy within yourself. By meeting your opponent with greater understanding than before you no longer hold fast to her through the one-sided, exaggerated and dark image in your soul. In this way you can give the enemy – who was, as it were, killed within your soul because you did not trust that she could develop any further – the gift of resurrection through forgiveness. Such a moral sacrifice helps both the receiver and the giver of the gift!

(1) Critical review at the end of the day[1]

You can use this method to get to know yourself better, even when you are not involved in conflict. Before going to sleep, recall the different events of the day, ideally in reverse order: look at what you did just before starting the review, then the situation before that, continuing until you reach the moment when you woke up in the morning.

The following visualization (Figure 3.1) will make this process easier: at the beginning of the review imagine you are climbing a hill near where you live and, from the top of the hill, from a greater distance, you look down on what you did during the day, as if it had happened several years ago rather than on that day.

On the top of your imaginary hill, ask yourself the following questions:
- What seems important about the day?
- What must now be considered more of a waste of time?
- When did I have difficulty mastering the tensions between my Everyday Ego and the Higher Self or the Shadow?
- When and how did I give my Higher Self space to develop?
- When and how did I give in to the urges of my Double?
- What were the influencing factors in this? What led me to pay more attention to my Double than to my Higher Self? And what helped me to pay more attention to my Higher Self?
- What unintentional consequences did my behaviour have?

Figure 3.1: Daily review

These are a few questions which can help you to put into practice what has been discussed so far, and to check your own behaviour from a self-critical distance. However, when carrying out this review, you must not try to interpret the day's events intellectually. It's enough to allow the images you remember to pass through your mind. A daily retrospective of this kind creates the basic attitude for many of the other exercises and methods: the review is the beginning of a distanced dialogue with yourself; you do not suppress certain events and you do not provoke, or justify yourself to, anyone else or make anyone else justify their actions.

(2) Inventory of your own ideals and values, strengths and positive moral characteristics

Spend about half an hour thinking about the values and goals that motivate you in your working and in your private life. This will give you direct access to your own values and ideals. The questions in Figure 3.2 are answered by working on your own; later you could perhaps discuss them with someone you trust, who can provide ideas and critical feedback.

Answer the following questions by looking back over the past 12 months:

- What strengths did I show during that time?
- What abilities was I able to rely on in those 12 months?
- Which qualities do I think my good friends particularly appreciated in me during that time?
- Looking back, what am I most proud of?
- Which of the moral qualities that I showed during that time are particularly important to me, even if I was only able to begin to realize them?
- Which ideals do I want to realize over the next year or two?
- What small steps can I undertake tomorrow to advance in that direction?

---

*Figure 3.2: Exercise for recognizing your own values
and personal strengths*

The aim of this exercise is not to set yourself absolute and un-achievably high ideals for the rest of your life, but to try and find out which aspects you can bring into your daily actions straightaway, which of the values and characteristics point you a little towards your desired ideals. A realistic behavioural goal that can be achieved tomorrow and checked by concrete means is worth more than a speculative goal for humankind that floats way above the clouds.

Particularly in small things – mostly unnoticed by other people – you can develop more of these qualities than through excessively demanding ideals which stretch you too far and will only discourage you.

(3) Uncovering buried values and ideals[2]
Often people do not succeed at uncovering their own values and ideals because they have been buried by their life experience and can therefore be accessed only indirectly. Rudolf Steiner gives an idea for a very effective method (Figure 3.3) of achieving this in his explanation relating to the 'mission of anger'.[3]

Use the following questions in your search for buried values and ideals:
1. What were the external events in my life between the ages of 18 and 24 approximately: what did I do in that time? How calm or unsettled does this period now appear to me in retrospect?
2. Which events during that time evoked stronger feelings and emotions than others?
3. Searching my memory for moments between the ages of 18 and 24 that caused me great indignation or anger, which episodes spring to mind? What happened at that time? How did it make me feel? What caused the indignation?

Important note: Indignation here denotes feelings of great anger in the sense of the emotion that is called 'holy anger' in the Bible: this 'holy' anger arises in people when other people violate their deepest sense of value.

Reconstruct such moments as precisely as possible and recall them in such a way that they evoke vivid emotional memories. If strong emotions arise when you think back over situations in which you experienced anger, then you have 'struck gold'.
Try to recall these situations vividly in your mind's eye.

4. Are there similarities between the different events?
5. Once you have looked at the different events, think about which values they challenged in you at that time. What is the common denominator? It is useful to formulate sentences such as 'I couldn't bear the fact that animals ...' or 'I was deeply shocked that foreign colleagues were ...' etc.
6. Finally look at later years, up until the present: where did I encounter the same values at a later time? When did I experience similar feelings – perhaps in a weaker form than around the age of 20?

Figure 3.3: Exercise to uncover buried values[4]

These questions elicit feelings about values that may have been forgotten. Therefore this method is particularly useful when the Everyday Ego has already become somewhat separated from the Higher Self.

Finally, the same method can also be used in relation to my conflict partners. Afterwards it may even be possible to have a conversation with them to talk about our values and non-values (see Chapter 6).

(4) Searching for similarities with your enemy
In conflict situations most people tend to overestimate and overemphasize the differences between themselves and their opponents and enemies. After all, they don't want to have anything in common with them! The following exercise can open your eyes to possible projections of your own weaknesses onto your opponent (Figure 3.4).

Honestly and conscientiously ask yourself the following questions:
- Which characteristics and patterns of behaviour do I find particularly objectionable in my enemy?
- Being completely honest, which characteristics and patterns of behaviour do I like least in myself?
- Which characteristics of my opponent are similar to my own negative characteristics?
- How have I handled my negative characteristics so far?
- When and how have I been able to improve something about myself – when and how did I not succeed?
- Do I know how my opponent tries to deal with her negative characteristics?

Figure 3.4: Exercise for discovering similarities with my enemy

Initially this search for similarities with the enemy mostly evokes dislike. But it is beneficial to carry on with it (Figure 3.5): the more you search for parallels, the more similarities you will discover. Often you will find more than you were prepared to admit to at first.

Now you can answer the next set of questions about similarities with your enemy:
- How do I respond to the unpleasant characteristics of my enemy? (Collect some behavioural patterns that are typical for you.)
- Have I made it clear to my enemy that I object to these characteristics? If so, how did I point this out?
- Was my enemy able to understand my pointers? If so, how did I know this?
- Could I give my signals in such a way that my opponent opened up to them? How did I achieve this?
- Conversely, to what extent has my opponent pointed out to me any shortcomings that she dislikes about me? How was this done?
- How did I feel about these pointers? What feelings did this evoke in me? Was I able to accept these pointers?

- How did I respond to these pointers? What did my reactions look like?
- Next time, could I respond to my opponent's pointers in different ways? Which behavioural patterns might be more suitable?

Figure 3.5: Exercise for recognizing enemy signals

These questions, too, are best worked on in an exchange with someone you trust.

(5) Checking interlocking with the opponent[5]

Each party in a conflict will usually think that she herself does not contribute to an escalation of the conflict, that she only responds to the opponent's provocations. But you might ask yourself to what extent you allow certain behavioural patterns by the opponent to provoke reactions in you that would not have occurred under normal circumstances (Figure 3.6). If you discover in yourself how you allow yourself to be provoked into uncontrolled behaviour, then you can control yourself better.

The following questions can help you to check interlocking between you and your opponent:

- Which behaviour by the opponent provoked me to such an extent that I lost self-control?
- What feelings did this behaviour evoke in me?
- To what extent did I allow my opponent to provoke me to act in a way where I was unable to foresee all the consequences?
- Conversely, what about my behaviour might have provoked reactions in my opponents that she was not quite in control of?

Figure 3.6: Checking interlocking with the opponent

In other words, to what extent do you continually condition each other without realizing? If you succeed at breaking the vicious cycle of mutual conditioning, you have found an important approach to solving the conflict as a whole.

(6) Searching for 'golden moments' in the opponent's behaviour – or: 'Michael and the dragon'[6]

The aim of this method is to enable you as a conflict party (at escalation level 4 and 5) to regain a sense of the opponent's personality as a whole. You need to do this exercise (Figure 3.7) on your own, without the other conflict party.

As an external adviser I also use this method when mediating between the conflict parties, but initially I always ask the opponents to work through it separately; if this has been positive, they can then – in the presence of a professional consultant – exchange results and report on what they have found out from each other.

Here are the steps to go through for recognizing 'golden moments'.

Select *two to four episodes* which have played an important part in intensifying the conflict. Recall these events in outline.

1. From the episodes you have identified, pick out *several moments (1–3)* where your opponent did not exclusively follow her negative urges but where you were able to see that she in some way *tried to follow her conscience* and to check her aggression.
2. For the *first moment you selected*, describe *specifically* and in detail how you remember your opponent's behaviour; also recall the room, the temperature, the colours, the light etc.
3. For the *second moment you selected*, describe *specifically* and in detail what you remember. Do the same for *the third moment* etc.
4. Now examine all these moments for the noticeable *positive intentions* and efforts and *turn this into a positive personality*, i.e. a figure from a fairy tale, fable, myth or similar. This figure will personify the positive aspects of the opponent.
5. Now pick out the most important *negative characteristics* and behaviours that you think you recognized in your opponent in the moments you described. Turn this into a *second, negative figure*. It may be useful to ask someone you trust to help with this, pointing out characteristics they noticed in the moments you described.

6. Finally get the *two opposing figures to talk to each other and to interact*. In this way you will create an encounter between the two figures – an adventure. The story of the two figures will tell itself, arising from the dynamics of the conflict and the character of the figures.
7. Once you have *told yourself the whole story, commit the images to your memory*. It is useful to remind yourself of this story before you go to bed or in other quiet moments, and to let it pass before your mind's eye.

Figure 3.7: 'Golden moments' exercise

I call these moments 'golden' because they allow you to perceive the actions of the Higher Self in your opponent. If you are able to recall these moments in the form of images, you will be better able to recognize these 'golden moments' in your opponent when you are next face-to-face. Then you will see the opponent holistically and, by recognizing how her Everyday Ego is wrestling with her Light and Shadow, you will no longer reduce him to a mere Shadow.

At the same time this method will make you more aware of your own wrestling with your Light and Shadow.

3.2 You can release the enemy within yourself

So what is the purpose of these small exercises? If you do them repeatedly, you should be able to develop a different view of your opponent and of yourself. This view looks at people as a whole, not just at aspects of their Double, which are subconsciously filtered out and enlarged in conflict situations.

The beneficial effect for your conflict arises from the fact that you are once again able to see the opponent wrestling with the daily tension between both her Everyday Ego and the Higher Self on the one hand, and the Everyday Ego and the Double on the other. In conflict situations the parties reduce each other to mere 'animals' and can hardly perceive 'the other' or 'the others' in any other way. Your behaviour also conditions and fixates your opponent in this way. However, by doing this you block your opponent – and your-self – from developing further. You do not grant her the capability to change for the better. Conflict parties usually think that the other person 'is like this and will remain so for eternity'. So they have already mentally written off the other person.

By approaching a conflict with the positive basic attitude of self-confrontation you can release the opponent or the enemy from this fixation. She can be 'resurrected' within you.

If this positive development continues in the relationship between the conflict parties, the former enemies may even reach the view that they could actually learn from each other. After all, through the confrontation in the conflict they have begun – although from a different motivation – to confront each other with challenges which may subsequently provide a stimulus for personal development.

The happiest experiences in my work as an adviser in conflict situations included occasions when former enemies reached the conclusion that they helped each other gain a more realistic view of themselves. If this can be achieved, both parties can benefit from the conflict: they arrive at a more comprehensive understanding of their own personality and a greater human depth in encounters with others. The painful but existential experiences of the conflict will have brought them a big step further in their self-knowledge and development, opening the way for their Everyday Ego to create a constructive relationship with their Higher Self and their Double.

3.3 How can I work on the tension between Light and Shadow within groups?

The exercises in Figures 3.8 to 3.13, drawn from the repertoire of organizational development methods I practise, deal with the clarification of the Light and Shadow personalities of a group, community or organization. They can be used by a group on its own, i.e. without external professional help, as long as the conflicts have not reached escalation level 4 (see Chapter 5).

(1) Developing a positive vision: the 'Light' personality of the group

Long-term goals and visions draw on the inspiring power of images (Figure 3.8), as evidenced in the description of a long-term goal as a 'guiding image'. Apart from addressing the intellect, images also appeal to people's feelings and will.

The following questions can first be answered individually; then the answers are exchanged and, through discussion, the group determines upon which points there is agreement:

1. If a good fairy granted me three wishes,
   - Where would I like to live in about 10 to 12 years?
   - Which colleagues would I like to work with?
   - For which customers (clients, pupils etc.) would I like to work?
2. What about this would be special, unique, attractive for me?
3. If I could set up my own group (company, school etc.) to do this, without having to consider finances or what has gone before,
   - What name would I choose for this community?
   - Which logo would go best with this? (Write/draw name and logo on a piece of paper)
4. What slogans or advertising messages would this group use to tell the outside world how it sees itself? In what way would it have to be unique and different from other groups (companies, schools etc.)?
5. Which three guiding principles should govern the internal co-operation of this group?
6. What do I absolutely want to avoid because it runs contrary to my values?
7. In what respect would it require courage for me to practise these ideas consistently, both internally and externally? What would I have to stop doing in order to be able to realize these ideas?

Figure 3.8: Working out a vision for the group:
'Our dream for the future' [7]

This method can help to make visible the Light personality shared by the group identity, and to enable people to discuss it. However, looking only at the ideal side can easily foster illusions. Therefore it is good – vital in conflict situations – to make visible the Shadow personality of the group identity as well.

(2) Profile of the group personality: Light and Shadow of a group

The following method (Figure 3.9) again uses the power of images. An organization such as a company, school, hospital etc. is viewed as a 'personality' and described in profile form, capturing both the positive characteristics and the Shadow sides of the group.

The profile of the everyday identity of a group is drawn up in a collective brainstorming exercise. Individual members of the group describe as clearly as possible the various objects or attributes which they consider typical for the personification of the organization. One person writes these characteristic descriptions on a flipchart. It does not matter if there are contradictions between different people's images – unless someone corrects or adds to their own image as a result of another person's contribution.

First agree whether the personality is a man or a woman. Roughly how old is he or she? Collect specific descriptions in the following areas:

Mr/Mrs (name of the organization, age, e.g. *Mrs Erasmus School, 55 years of age ...*)

1. ... lives in the following house/the following flat and in the following area: *(e.g. 1950s bungalow, painted white with a grey roof; on the outskirts of a town, with lots of greenery around/between blocks of flat; with a small, neglected garden; the house has small windows ...)*

2. ... has furnished the house/flat in the following way: *(e.g. hallway with a coat rack made of rattan; oak dining table, in bad taste; large TV set dominates the room ...)*

3. ... has the following acquaintances/friends: *(e.g. colleagues; old school friends; trendy painter; street musicians, rope dancer ...)*

4.   ... likes to eat: *(e.g. English food, roast beef and Yorkshire pudding; tea; occasionally goes for a pub lunch ...)*
5.   ... likes to wear: *(e.g. loose clothes; old jeans, suits; trendy scarf thrown over one shoulder ...)*
6.   ... has the following hobbies: *(e.g. crosswords; coach tours to the West Country; gardening – growing vegetables ...)*
7.   ... uses the following means of transport: *(e.g. dark grey Rover; bicycle; bus and tram ...)*
8.   Add one or two points you think are important to describe the personality.

Figure 3.9: 'Personality' profile of the group[8]

The ideal group size for this exercise is six to eight people. If the group is larger, it can be divided into smaller teams which will do the exercise in parallel; the profiles are then presented to the whole group and discussed:

- Which characteristics do we agree on?
- Where are the contradictions? What do the contradictions tell us about the 'personality' of the group?
- Which objects, attributes, characteristics of the personality we have described are we least happy with? Can we look at these together in more detail?

The image elements of such a profile will elicit both likeable and unlikeable characteristics. The least satisfactory objects and attributes can now be condensed into another personality, which makes visible the Double of the organization described. These characteristics are also written down on a flipchart and condensed into a portrait. It is fine if humour comes into play during this exercise. However, there is great danger of a cynical tone developing while gathering such characteristics. If this happens, it is important to ensure that individual group members are not personally mocked or insulted.

(3) Goals for changing the group identity: the path from Shadow into Light

Once the profiles have been presented, they can be used to determine the direction of desired changes. How this can be done is described in Figure 3.10.

After presentation of the profile the group discusses the following questions, still using metaphors for items 1 to 3:

1. Which things (house/flat, furniture, vehicle etc.) do we want to change so that guests of the personality described will be able to feel at ease in the house for some time? *(E.g. we want to enlarge the small windows and remove the dark, heavy curtains; we want to pull down partitions between some small rooms etc.)*

2. Which patterns of behaviour (eating, hobbies etc.) should the personality described change so that, as guests, we would feel at ease with her? *(E.g. we want to celebrate special days with an elegant meal; no more junk food; no organized coach trips but an adventure holiday etc.)*

3. What should be changed in the friendships of the person described so that we feel we could be part of her circle of friends? *(E.g. we want to include Africans amongst our friends; musicians should also become part of our circle etc.)*

4. Finally the desired changes can create a profile of the desired personality.

5. Now the metaphors are unravelled: what exactly needs to happen in order to translate the images from the responses to 1 to 3 into reality? *(E.g. enlarging windows means focusing more on the external environment, visiting seminars, having closer contact with customers etc.)*

Figure 3.10: Desired changes in the profile image

This discussion will throw up some controversies, but it is useful to discuss the images in the group and to investigate which guiding ideas and values they express. When doing this, it is equally important to explore what should be avoided.

(4) Directional statements to overcome the tension between Light and Shadow

The existing tension between Light and Shadow in the identity of the group can be made more beneficial, as shown in Figure 3.10. The methods shown in Figures 3.8, 3.9 and 3.10 form the basis for this work.

Summarize the essence of the Light and Shadow image of your group (school, hospital, company etc.) in tight statements to produce the following declarations of intent, e.g.:

We want to get away from ...	and we want to move towards ...
• indirect forms of communication	• direct and honest communication
• the formation of impenetrable cliques	• transparent lines of decision-making
• a climate of reproaches and moral appeals	• a climate of open confrontation and discussion
• etc. ...	• etc. ...

Figure 3.11: Binding directional statements to overcome the Shadow identity

Good intentions which cannot be kept in some situations poison the atmosphere. Therefore you should describe both the direction in which the group wants to develop and what it wants to move away from. To illustrate the effect of this technique, think of the Israelites moving out of Egypt: when the image of the promised land faded in the minds of the people during their long walk through the desert, Moses was able to encourage them to carry on by reminding them of the hardships of the country they had left. When realizing the ideals of its community, every group generally embarks on a long and difficult journey. If there is a danger that the community may lose sight of its destination, remembering where the group came from and where it wants to get to can help it regain focus.

This method of directional statements can also be used to reach a group consensus for joint work on conflict, or for seeking external conflict consultancy.

(5) Discussing discrepancies between ideal and reality in the group: 'delta analysis'

In working groups or organizations that are committed to demanding religious, ideological, political or other ideals, the risk of conflict is often particularly great. People generally join these groups for particular reasons and expect everyone in the group to do their best to live commonly held ideals. As already shown in Chapter 2, this can lead to 'positive idolization' tipping over into 'negative idolization'[9] as soon as common ideals are no longer lived consistently within everyday routine. Therefore a group should learn to discuss such discrepancies constructively very early on.

In many churches, alternative schools, progressive political parties and humanitarian voluntary organizations this creates a problematic culture, since it involves dangerous taboos: on the one hand, the higher the expectations individual group members have of the group, the deeper disappointments will run; on the other hand there is often an unwritten law that disappointments and mistakes must *not* be discussed. Group members are frightened that they might be blamed if they disturb the peaceful – if only apparently peaceful – working of the group by bringing up these problems. And they prefer not to carry this guilt. Therefore they internalize their discomfort – and this escalates into destructive negative idolization. This is particularly pronounced when each member of the group thinks she is devoting all her physical and psychological energy to the group but does not perceive the same commitment from other group members. This leads to an attitude of silent reproach – but this cannot be concealed from the other group members for long. After a while such frustration is expressed in moralizing remarks and demands.

Therefore suitable forms need to be developed to enable group members to deal constructively with personal criticism and personal acknowledgement. Two things need to be learned:

a)   how to formulate mutual recognition for all the *positive things* individuals have achieved for the group and how this can be expressed within the group; and

b)   how group members should go about discussing *critical points* in the behaviour of colleagues or employees.

The two points are closely related: if I am convinced that I have given everything to the group, without ever receiving acknow-ledgement or recognition for it, then after a while I will experience this as an imbalance in the relationship – and therefore as unfair-ness. 'Other group members do wrong because we do not work together under the same conditions! I sacrifice myself for the group while others make themselves an easy life. They are actually exploiting me.' There are many groups in which practically all members feel the same way, that they are misunderstood by everyone else, treated unfairly and exploited – even if they appear patient and modest on the surface.

This feeling gradually turns into bitterness and eventually culminates in a hardening of the soul. For a while these feelings are suppressed – but eventually the accumulated pressure becomes too great and discharges itself in surprisingly explosive actions. Therefore, in order to prevent conflict, organizations should periodically seek to make visible what people have achieved and how much they are able to achieve. This transparency in itself will achieve a certain amount of recognition. Figure 3.12 shows several ways to do this.

These and similar exercises should be carried out regularly as they can help to prevent the emergence of conflicts aggravated by neglect.

Preventative measures are also better for discussing perceived discrepancies between ideal and reality than are 'curative measures' used after the event. Figure 3.13 shows some possibilities for achieving this.

A culture of mutual personal acknowledgement can be created in the following way:

1. **Review of contributions made:** at the end of the year there is a review, in groups of three or four, of what was achieved in that period; the following points should be discussed:
   - During this time, what did I want to do over and above, or in a better way, than during earlier periods?
   - During this time, where did I want to do less, or what did I no longer want to do, in order to reduce the pressure I am under?
   - How did I perceive my workload in comparison with other people's? When did this cause me a problem?
   - What are my goals for the coming period? Where do I want to set my personal limits?

   The small groups can agree to discuss the resolutions they have made for the coming period, and to support one another in the implementation of these resolutions. Basic questions about equality or inequality that arise in the small group discussions can be brought to the whole group.

2. **Inventory of resources:** Once a year a group discussion is held to list what additional capabilities members will offer – over and above the performance that is routinely expected. To do this, each group member first spends a few minutes thinking about what she wants to offer, writes this down on index cards, goes up to the flipchart and displays her cards for all to see. All group members present what they want to offer in the same way, and the group discusses what is actually needed. Then – and only then – people commit themselves publicly by going back to the flipchart and signing their own cards to show that they feel bound to their offer.

3. **Trusted group:** A group is set up for a fixed period of time with the task of talking to people as soon as these people or others signal that there is a problem.

Figure 3.12: Giving recognition for achievement

As a group, you can agree to have a discussion devoted only to the following questions:

1. Which values and ideals are particularly important to you? Ask each group member to write down the three most important ideals she thinks should be lived in the group.
2. Collect these statements and, in the group, cluster the same or similar ideals, i.e. record which ideals are related to others and which stand on their own.
3. Working together, rank these ideals in order of importance, e.g. by giving each person two green dots to identify her most important ideals.
4. Take another look at these prioritized ideals: which are likely to be the most difficult to put into practice in everyday life? To do this, give each person two red dots and talk about what is likely to make them so difficult to achieve.
5. Discuss the ideals that are most difficult to achieve, ideally in small groups:
   – Why are these ideals so difficult to achieve?
   – What do I personally find most difficult?
   – What help would I like in this from other group members?
6. What should we agree to do to prevent possible discrepancies from leading to disappointments and reproaches? What should not happen? What will we do if it does happen?
7. The group results are presented to the whole group, discussed, agreed and written down. A date is agreed to review progress in relation to these agreements.

Figure 3.13: Preview of likely discrepancies between ideal and reality

If the behaviour of individual group members has already led to disappointment, methods as described in Chapter 1 can be very useful. It is always important to give direct feedback in the form of 'I-messages', statements formulated in the first person, to say what feelings were caused in you and how you perceive the behaviour that has led to disappointment.

Chapter 6 includes further possibilities of this kind.

4. How conflicts are driven

Intense conflicts do not materialize out of thin air; they gradually become more intense. But as many people prefer to avoid conflict, they often overlook the first signals, only facing the situation when quite a lot has happened. This can be illustrated in the following examples of a factory and a school:

For some time the atmosphere in Plant 3 of **'Boilerworks plc'** *had been so heavy that it could have been cut with a knife; then, all of a sudden, the situation reached crisis point: the maintenance mechanics were no longer prepared to put up with the 'crazy things' going on in the plant and decided on a wild-cat strike, which temporarily paralysed production.*

After many confusing and tiring debates amongst the teaching staff of the **'Erasmus School'** *the head teacher was suddenly accused of manipulating the school finances and maliciously deceiving parents and staff. The situation could not continue and the head teacher was to leave the school immediately.*

A great deal must have been attempted and must have failed for a team of mechanics to risk shutting down a factory. And teachers do not suddenly accuse a head teacher of criminal offences unless other things have already gone wrong. Conflicts escalate successively, they move downhill level by level, possibly even plunging into the abyss.

4.1 Thresholds of escalation

Before each level of escalation we can experience a *threshold*, which asks us to think again, to pause, or to go back. Figure 4.1 lists questions we can ask of ourselves in order to prevent being drawn further into the maelstrom of events.

Are you in a situation of tension with other people? If so, please answer the following questions honestly:

1. Do I really want to go that far?
2. Do I still have control of myself?
3. Can I see the effects of my actions? Can I imagine the un-intentional side effects of my actions as well?
4. Am I really prepared to take on the consequences of my actions and omissions? Do I want to take responsibility for them?

Figure 4.1: Questions of conscience at the conflict thresholds

Most people intuitively recognize these thresholds. They know that if they do not keep themselves under control, a lot will be destroyed and it may be impossible to trust one another ever again. Because of this intuitive knowledge of escalation thresholds, the people involved will restrain themselves – at least for a while – and will not risk everything straightaway. Therefore a conflict does not turn into complete destruction immediately but intensifies successively, unless something is done about it. These thresholds represent warning signals, to shake up people's awareness, and they have a protective function. We can recognize and respect them, and can look for other forms of handling the conflict, enlist the help of others or seek professional help. Alternatively we can ignore these threshold signals. This happens either in blind anger, from stubbornness or defiance: 'Right, that's it! Now I'll show him!'

So thresholds offer the conflict parties an opportunity which they can seize or which they can ignore. It is up to them whether they are 'beside themselves' or, instead, 'with themselves', thinking, feeling, wanting and acting from within their own Ego. There is always one vital question for people involved in conflict: are their actions self-directed or other-directed? Being other-directed can mean that they are not acting in full consciousness, instead responding more or less unthinkingly to the actions of their opponents. This is what thresholds point to.

If a conflict has been brewing for a substantial period of time, it is useful to ask yourself some of the following questions (Figure 4.2). This will help to distil individual critical episodes which become keys for freeing up the conflict.

---

1. Starting from today, I look back over the history of the conflict so far: in retrospect, which moments or events evoke strong feelings of displeasure or anger, of pain or confusion? Where am I still confused about the course of events?
2. When exactly did each episode occur? Identify dates as precisely as possible, e.g.
    (1) on April 15 at 3.40pm,
    (2) on March 15 at 9.45am,
    (3) on February 7 at 11.20am
    (4) etc.
3. What was destroyed or lost in the events identified? What became noticeably worse afterwards? How had it been before?
    On (1): *Afterwards:* Since that time I have suspected my opponent, Anne, of systematically lying to us. She has no longer respected the good reputation of the school. *Before:* Mutual respect for honour; fear that people might begin to talk about the school.
    On (2): *Afterwards:* Gossip about Anne behind her back; enlisting support for my point of view by... *Before:* Constant attempts at talking to seek clarification about the controversial topics.
    On (3): etc.
4. Which critical episodes might my opponent identify from his point of view?

Figure 4.2: Identifying critical episodes in a conflict

4.2 What drives escalation?

When there are differences of opinion, it can become more difficult to talk to one another and tensions can arise. People then become stressed, are somewhat impatient and annoyed in the way they respond to one another and thus cause new anger, which in turn leads to aggressive reactions – in words and deeds. This can be the start of a tension that can quickly give rise to a conflict that has a dynamic all of its own: an interplay of vicious circles of 'self-intensification' and 'self-infection', as shown in Chapter 1.

From the first, minor differences right through to the most intense levels of escalation, there are a number of driving mechanisms which continue to add new fuel to the conflict. This driving forward is largely unnoticed by the people involved. I talk about mechanisms because they automatically cause effects that people are not conscious of, and as Figure 4.3 shows, these driving mechanisms are paradoxically linked and intensify one another.

A.1 **Snowballing of contentious issues:** More and more issues are thrown into the disagreement; infection of issues

and simultaneously …

A.2 **Increasing simplification** in taking up the opposing party's issues: 'Anthony clearly cares about one thing only...!'

B.1 **Widening of the arena:** More and more people are drawn into the argument; the circle of involvement is extended; the interests of many people/groups are collectivized and mixed up.

and simultaneously …

B.2 **Increasing personification:** 'Anthony is the cause of all evil!' 'Get rid of Anthony!'

C.1 **Pessimistic anticipation:** I am prepared for the worst possible scenario: 'Things are always worse than you think!'

and simultaneously …

C.2 **Self-fulfilling prophecy:** Through my actions I create the situation I wanted to avoid!

Figure 4.3: Paradoxically linked driving mechanisms of escalation

These mechanisms are described in more detail and illustrated in the following sections.

A.1 Snowballing of contentious issues – and simultaneously
A.2 Increasing simplification

During the course of the argument the conflict parties bring in more and more issues. This is illustrated by the following examples from the factory and the school.

*Initially the **mechanics** on strike complained that:*
- *they always had to be at the ready,*
- *their working hours were completely erratic;*

later the following were added:
- *their pay is far below what is usual,*
- *working conditions in the factory are poor,*
- *management is erratic;*

then they complained that:
- *their interests always come last,*
- *everybody bosses them about as if they are slaves etc.*

*The 'progressive' **teachers** initially discussed:*
- *the use of suitable teaching aids,*
- *the didactical theory of 'learning by discovery';*

later the issues were extended to:
- *questions of the democratic leadership of the school,*
- *the limits of the teachers' decision-making powers,*
- *the involvement of parents in the school;*

finally their conflict also covered:
- *the position of the school within the town,*
- *the role of the school within the educational system etc.*

In this way the number of issues increased and at the same time the conflict shifted to completely different questions. The mechanics and teachers did this consciously to some extent, because they did actually see a connection between the issues, but also with the simple intention of strengthening their position. However, to some extent this was also an unconscious process because opposing arguments led them to switch to issues they believed would provide 'ammunition'. Conscious and unconscious processes work together. On the other hand the opposing sides in the factory and the school were completely certain that most of the arguments that were advanced were merely meant to fudge, or distract from, the 'main issue':

Company **management** *was wondering what all the to-ing and fro-ing was supposed to achieve and was convinced that the mechanics on strike were only interested in getting more money!*

The 'conservative' **head teacher** *was certain that all the 'progressives' wanted was to be thought 'trendy' by the pupils!*

The events can be summarized as follows: when speaking, Party A wants to extend the issues; while listening, Party B wants to keep an overview by simplifying matters. What is fatal is that, when speaking, Party B also contributes to the snowballing effect and, when listening, Party A responds by simplifying in order to keep an overview and to stick by its position. Whenever one party throws in an argument, the other party feels misunderstood or feels that the subtlety of the issues is ignored, as they receive only un-differentiated answers to their differentiated arguments. The longer this goes on, the more frequently the parties miss each other's points. When mounting anger feeds suspicion, the conflict parties increasingly suspect the other side of doing all this deliberately.

If you think you have been involved in an escalating conflict for some time, the questions in Figure 4.4 can help you to clarify your own point of view.

Honestly answer the following questions about your conflict:

1. What were the issues for me initially?
   The issues were A, B and C.

2. What issues were added later? A1, A2, C1, C2, C3, D and E. Which were dropped?

3. Were other new issues added later? Were any dropped?
   A3, C4, E1 and E2 as well as F and G were added.
   A2 and B were dropped.

4. Show the linkages between the issues in a 'tree diagram':

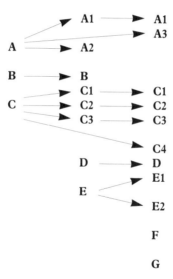

5. Try to show the changes in the issues of the opposing party as you see them, in a similar way.

6. Compare the two 'tree diagrams': where are the overlaps? where are the gaps?

Figure 4.4: Self-diagnosis questions about the
snowballing of contentious issues

B.1 Widening of the arena – and simultaneously
B.2 Increasing personification

There is a tendency in conflicts to widen the arena (often called the 'theatre of war') in which the arguments are conducted. In this mechanism, too, Party A will tend to draw more people into the argument to support its position, whilst Party B is completely convinced that there are only a few people, the 'troublemakers', pulling the strings behind the scenes.

Initially the **mechanics** *had only conducted their arguments with their line manager, then they asked to speak to their line manager's boss; when they took strike action, the differences became visible to the rest of the factory; at the same time the strikers tried to win the other employees over to their side; eventually they sought support from the trade union.*

At the beginning of the differences the **teachers** *had had heated debates within their subject groups; later the arguments included the management team of the school; next a meeting involved all the teaching staff; soon the pupils were also entangled in the conflict, and before long the parents also had to take sides.*

Management *in the factory suspected that a particular mechanic, who had unsuccessfully applied for a management position, stood behind all the actions.*

The **head teacher** *was sure of one thing: his deputy, who wanted to increase his public profile at any price, was the ringleader.*

One further mechanism contributes to the personification of conflict: the attacks shift *from the deed to the culprit*.[1] In our examples this means:

Management *in the factory*
- *first complains about some mistakes in a repair carried out by the team of mechanics that later goes on strike (**deed**);*
- *later speaks of the 'bad repairs' in general carried out by the team of mechanics;*
- *later criticizes them publicly: 'the work of the mechanics' team is always rubbish';*
- *eventually describes the mechanics as 'idiots' (**culprits**)!*

The head teacher *of the school*
- *first criticizes some short-comings in the teaching methods of the young teachers who see themselves as 'progressive' (**deed**);*
- *later says that the teaching methods of the young teachers 'leave a lot to be desired';*
- *after a while frequently remarks that the young teachers' lessons are poor;*
- *finally labels the young teachers as 'failures' (**culprits**).*

As with the snowballing effect, increasing generalization in judgements about people leads those involved to feel unfairly judged, or even prejudged. They reject these judgements and want to show that the other party, not they themselves, are really the 'trouble-makers'. So the tables are turned. Figure 4.5 offers some questions for self-critical examination.

---

1. When was the circle of people actively involved in the conflict abruptly widened?
2. Who was drawn in by me or my party?
3. Did these people bring new issues and interests into the conflict?
4. Who was drawn in by the other party?
5. Did these people bring new issues and interests into the conflict?
6. Are there any signs that our side tends to shift the negative judgement 'from the deed to the culprit'? What could I do about this?
7. Are there any signs that the opposing side tends to shift the negative judgement 'from the deed to the culprit'? What could I do about this?
8. How can the situation created by widening the arena be kept under control?

Figure 4.5: Questions on the widening of the arena

In advanced stages of conflict it is not easy to answer these questions impartially. If they are answered in conjunction with other people, it should repeatedly become obvious how much the views differ – this is the nature of conflicts. Chapter 1 has already shed some light on this.

C.1 Pessimistic anticipation – and simultaneously
C.2 Self-fulfilling prophecy

When the tensions increase, mutual suspicion will also grow. People accuse each other of having worse motives than they actually show. And to ensure that they do not end up looking weaker or more stupid, they would rather have too much than too little ammunition before they venture into the conflict arena. Thus the dynamics of escalating conflict are determined by a tendency to oversensitivity, to overarmament and overreaction, as described in the 'Richardson process of the arms race'.[2]

*When the **team of mechanics** went on strike, they feared that they would not be taken completely seriously. Therefore they decided to announce the news about the strike straightaway (which to begin with would involve a rather complicated machine whose down-times would cause higher costs), and to present management with a list of hard demands.*

*The young **teachers** raised their issues with massive protest in the weekly staff meeting; in order to get everyone's attention, they decided to interrupt an ongoing discussion of a different topic, express protest against the authoritarian and repressive chair of the meeting and use the resulting confusion to get their points put on the agenda immediately.*

The management team was surprised at this 'heavy ammunition'; they reacted strongly and this triggered a more militant approach:

After their first clashes with the surprised management team, the **mechanics** *on strike decided to shut down an even more complicated machine and added some more, particularly weighty demands to their original list.*

Because of the 'authoritarian, repressive reaction' of the head teacher, the protesting **teachers** *deviated from their original plan, left the meeting under loud protest and decided to go on strike the next day.*

In both situations the very thing occurred which the attacking parties had initially not wanted at all. When they were preparing their approach, they had considered the possibility of greater resistance. But when the opposing party did not give way, as they had hoped – 'Of course, nobody would have expected it from these managers' – they changed up a gear. However, this led to a different course of events than they had anticipated. Each threat holds a tendency to bring about the very circumstances the threat was meant to avert. This is the doomed paradox of threats.

In order to avoid sliding into a dead-end situation, it is useful to check one's own thinking and attitudes, as described in Figure 4.6.

Before I go into the next personal confrontation, I will ask myself the following questions:

1. Which of my actions might the opposing party see and misconstrue as a massive danger or threat?
2. What can I do to avoid such misunderstandings?
3. Which alternative actions are available to me to defuse the situation if my counterpart's reaction turns out to be much stronger or more violent than anticipated?
4. How can I show strength and decisiveness and still remain open to signals that my counterpart may be prepared to cooperate?

Figure 4.6: Preparing for a potentially confrontational encounter

This is the essence of all efforts: I must not become a prisoner of my own limited powers of imagination and must not manoeuvre myself into a dead-end situation that is hard to get out of. For if there is an opportunity to present my agenda clearly and unmistakably, there is also a danger that I might exaggerate to such an extent that my opponent rejects the very thing I want to achieve. And the opponent doesn't do this because he doesn't understand my arguments, but in response to my aggressive approach. This is the paradox: I became more aggressive precisely because I thought that otherwise I might not appear sufficiently convincing. But I overlook the fact that the aggression of my counterpart is not directed at the position I assume but at the aggressive manner in which I have presented my stance, as I was worried I might not be convincing enough.

5. How conflicts can go downhill

If you recognize the most important characteristics of the different levels of intensity in a conflict, you can do something about it in time:

- you can either prevent further, unwanted escalation,
- or you can consciously escalate the conflict further (or allow this to happen),
- or you yourself can find a constructive solution for the differences that exist,
- or, knowing that at the current level of escalation you are unable to get to grips with the problems yourself, you can seek external help.

As shown in Chapter 1, it all depends whether 'I have a conflict' or whether 'the conflict has me'. Having differences is the most natural thing in the world in human interaction; having differences doesn't mean there is conflict. Everything depends on how people handle those differences. The tension becomes a conflict when the people involved can no longer deal with it constructively.

The following description only covers the key characteristics of the levels of conflict.[1] They are a great help as 'landmarks' that show you where you are, provided you don't just pay attention to a few individual features but look at the overall pattern of characteristics. Individual features from later levels can occasionally appear earlier, but on their own they don't represent a certain level:

- On level 3 (actions, not words), for example, people sometimes make certain 'threats', as we saw in the case study of the mechanics on strike in the factory: 'We will hand in our notice if you don't suspend the new maintenance system immediately!' However, these should not be mistaken for the consciously used strategies of threats on level 6, which dominate events completely and which threaten the opposing party with lasting damage.

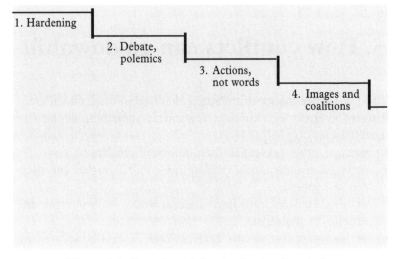

Figure 5.1: Overview of the nine levels of escalation

- Or: on level 4 (images and coalitions) the conflict parties allow themselves to be tempted into hurting each other with snide remarks. However, the relatively insignificant damage caused in this way bears no relation to the destructive blows of level 7, where the extent of the damage comes close to being an existential danger to the opponent.

Just as a red spot on the skin doesn't support a diagnosis of measles, an individual feature is not enough to correctly identify the escalation level. On every level of escalation the interplay of several mechanisms and characteristics contributes to an overall pattern which corresponds to the 'main formula' (e.g. 'actions, not words'). There must also be an element of 'chronification': the patterns repeat themselves and have a certain degree of permanence.

In contrast with other theories of escalation, I deliberately represent the gradual intensification of the conflict as a *downward* movement. The escalation goes 'deeper and deeper', not 'higher and higher', moving through nine levels. It progressively activates deeper and more subconscious levels, both in people and in groups, until these people or groups completely lose their self-control.

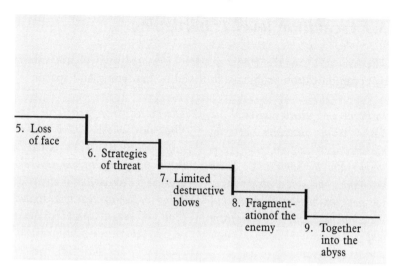

Therefore Figure 5.1 illustrates the escalation as steps leading downwards. At every step there is a threshold which can make people aware that they are about to cross over to the next lower level of escalation. The bold vertical lines symbolize these thresholds. The lower the level, the more intense and the more violent the fighting. The suction of the conflict mechanisms pulls the conflict further and further down, unless the conflict parties wake up and tackle this internal dynamic. However, this requires an understanding of the mechanisms, the ability to recognize what is happening, awareness and moral strength.

The following sections illustrate the main characteristics of the different levels of escalation, using the same two examples as the preceding chapter: the manufacturing company 'Boilerworks plc' and the alternative 'Erasmus School' in a large city. In order to protect the organizations whose conflicts are used as illustrative examples from being identified, the descriptions combine events from several similar cases. So the events are not fictional, they have actually happened.

5.1 Escalation level 1: hardening

The two scenarios show how this level is increasingly characterized by communication problems, followed by hardening and spasm.

*In Plant 3 of '**Boilerworks**' the daily team meetings of the maintenance section had been problematic for some time. Some mechanics had voiced objections to the new maintenance system, but these had been rejected by the team leader. The sessions became longer and longer because there was more and more to discuss. The discussions repeatedly went round in circles, and their outcomes were often vague. In subsequent sessions decisions already made were again put in question because there had been implementation problems.*

The team leader thought he had to respond to this with stricter chairing. He introduced a fixed agenda, restricted the time he allowed others to speak and often declared objections irrelevant. The mechanics went along with this unwillingly.

*The **teaching staff** of the 'Erasmus School' had a weekly staff meeting. When several pupils in the 6th form left, the teachers discussed curriculum matters. A group of young teachers argued that the young people should receive better tuition in the use of computers, but this was rejected by a group of older colleagues. The discussion was passionate and intense, though chaotic; arguments became extended and repetitive, but neither group was able to convince the other. Occasionally the tone became sharper, although this was immediately rectified by apologies and clarification. As the discussions had repeatedly been unsatisfactory, the staff decided to hold a special weekend session to discuss the subject.*

From time to time the stances taken in the disagreement harden, 'crystallize' and clash. The opponents can no longer be completely open towards each other; they develop internal reservations. Communication suffers because each side increasingly sees events as through a filter, i.e. they do not recognize things around them or filter them out; they listen and see only selectively. Those involved repeatedly oscillate between co-operation and competitiveness.

Therefore the discussions come to a temporary halt. But even if people occasionally become paralysed in their competitive attitudes, they will still try to get things going again. But as this already requires a certain amount of effort, there are repeated glitches. A paradoxical effect becomes apparent: people are aware of the glitches and tensions, but this very knowledge increasingly causes new spasm.

5.2 Escalation level 2: debate and polemics

As they cross the threshold to level 2, the opponents cease to listen to each other's arguments. Being right and presenting one's own position in a positive light has already become as important as the discussion of facts.

After several disruptions in the production process, the maintenance team leader accused some of his mechanics of having failed to adhere to his instructions for the work. He said that this had led to substantial production downtime. The mechanics defended themselves against these accusations, contrasting the old maintenance system – sophisticated and proven – with the new, badly designed system. They demanded that management should finally listen to reason. The team leader strongly rejected this.

Shortly afterwards, in a meeting of an interdepartmental project team concerned with customer focus, one of the mechanics spoke cynically about the problems with the new system

Before the weekend session there were heated debates in the subject groups, and in other forums, about IT teaching, the importance of creative subjects, personal development. The young 'Progressives' distributed a discussion paper in which they extended their demands and provided supporting arguments. The opposing party also produced a pamphlet with the title 'ProArt' in which, drawing on renowned pedagogical authorities, they refuted the arguments of the 'Progressives'. This was followed by a new, stronger pamphlet from the 'Progressives' in which they demanded 'an open school for the future' instead of a 'school for the past'.

The weekend session saw very emotional debates, without any sign of a solution. Instead, further

and argued for a open, co-operative leadership style in the organization.

In the next team meeting the team leader angrily picked up on that discussion, pulled the old system to shreds and insisted that everybody had to adhere to the new system 100%. He criticized the unfair form of debate he felt the mechanics were using.

controversial subjects were identi-fied, and these were to be discussed in the coming weeks:

- *suitable forms of address*
- *discipline during lessons*
- *smoking, alcohol and drugs at school*
- *art lessons vs. vocational training*
- *financial situation etc.*

At the beginning of the disagreement, different opinions and stances provided creativity, re-orientation, stimulation and life, because it seemed possible to resolve the differences in an objective, factual discussion. Now the opposing parties go to extremes in polarizing and cementing their stances. Through selective listening the weaknesses and mistakes in the opponents' arguments are quickly identified and refuted. Thinking, feeling and will slide into extremes, and the extreme positions appear mutually exclusive.

The disagreement is governed by pseudo-logical ways of thinking,[2] which can almost be equated with 'rational violence':

- The discussion is diverted to areas where people feel superior.
- Arguments are used in order to make the opposing party feel insecure on a psychological level.
- Causal connections are claimed to exist between facts merely because they followed one another chronologically, etc.

Each side is trapped in its own language and can no longer listen objectively to the concerns of the opposing side. An 'overtone' emerges in this language: this sounds correct and polite on the surface, but on closer listening includes hidden, aggressive 'undertones'. The different messages of 'overtone' and 'undertone' increasingly create contradictions and confusion.

The discussion is no longer alive and creative but becomes completely mechanistic: an argument is followed by a strong counter-argument, which in turn is followed by another counter-argument. It is an intellectual game of ping-pong, in which every side wants to show its intellectual superiority through polemic. There are many types of behaviour designed to impress, which shift attention from the original factual issues to the personal level. Uninvolved people are turned into an admiring audience – their applause can become more important to the people involved in the argument than the extent to which they can convince the opposing party. Co-operation and competitiveness alternate continuously and contribute to the confusion of the people and groups involved. However, the people involved still attempt to bridge their differences through talking.

Explanatory models such as those used in transaction analysis[3] make a valuable contribution towards an understanding of this level.

5.3 Actions, not words

Most of the many debates that have taken place ended in deadlock. Therefore the conflict parties no longer believe that they can reach and convince each other through words, nor that the differences that exist can be resolved through an exchange of views. On the contrary – they only irritate each other more by talking! Therefore they come to believe that 'Actions, not words, are the decisive factor'!

The meetings of the maintenance team continued to go badly. The mechanics had agreed amongst themselves to use the new system in a 'work to rule' initiative. Where this led to production problems, they would immediately take recourse to the rules of the old system, thus proving its superiority. The production managers got used to this approach and enlisted the

Despite several weekend sessions and conferences lasting several days during the Christmas and Easter holidays, there was less and less consensus. Enjoyment of the debate quickly dwindled. The proponents of both parties declared that, until a binding agreement was reached, they would do what best fitted in with their own convictions. The 'Progressives' allowed the pupils to eat and drink during

help of the maintenance team according to the old system.

The team leader brought fewer and fewer agenda items to the meetings, instead giving the mechanics his orders in an abrupt manner, without providing further reasons. The most articulate mechanic increasingly acted as a spokesman for the team in disagreements with the boss, and he organized informal team meetings without the manager.

lessons, to join them in an occasional cigarette in the schoolyard, to address them by their first name etc. The 'ProArt' group, on the other hand, demanded disciplined behaviour from the children during lessons, participation in all creative lessons, no smoking during break time etc. The atmosphere between the two parties was tense, and informal conversations became increasingly rare.

Each conflict party is simply doing what it is convinced of, presenting the opposing party with a *fait accompli*: 'If you don't listen to me, I shan't listen to you either!' As soon as actions govern events, the opponents regard each other with suspicion. If they recognize discrepancies between words and actions, their suspicion increases – and with it their inability to understand the other side. Therefore the messages of body language, non-verbal communication, play a key role on this level.[4]

If people mistrust what has been said, they may find meaning in the following order:

1. In discrepancies between content and vocal expression, the negative message of the voice is given more credence than the content.
2. When the vocal expression does not give a clear indication of whether somebody has evil intentions, their facial expression is given more credence than their voice.
3. If there is doubt about the honesty of the facial expression, the messages conveyed by the hands are considered more credible than those of the facial features,
4. ... and those of the body more than those of the hands,
5. ... and finally those of the legs and feet more than those of the rest of the body.

It should be noted that this shift in focus occurs when somebody makes the assumption that the other party is trying to hide potentially hostile intentions. Scepticism then leads to the 'downward shift' from 1 to 5, as described, as the negative intentions 'leak downwards'.

It is only at this point that people form real parties that close themselves off against the outside world, as if they were forming a layer of skin around themselves. They exclude elements that don't fit in: 'Birds of a feather flock together!' They experience an indeterminate sense of 'us'. Increasing internal group pressure[5] brings opinions and positions into line within the group (pressure to conform): 'Things are getting serious, so the interests of the group must take precedence over individual opinions!' Within the group tasks are now allocated less flexibly, as special roles emerge for certain people, who are repeatedly pushed into these roles, e.g. that of 'aggressor', 'foreign affairs secretary', 'guardian of goodwill' etc.

This is the key to all these changes: the conflict parties – whether they are individuals, groups, organizations or larger units – rapidly lose empathy. They become captives of their own emotions and can barely empathize with the feelings of others.

5.4 Escalation level 4: images and coalitions

With the next levels of escalation the psychological distance between the conflict parties increases dramatically. If so far they only objected to certain types of behaviour by the opponent, the different patterns perceived as typical now merge into an overall image of the conflict parties.

The team leader repeatedly challenged the mechanics about their 'work to rule' initiative, emphasizing that, as a manager, he was not prepared to put up with 'this kind of thing'. Moreover, he repeatedly said in conversations within the plant that he thought

The actions of the 'Progressives' and the 'ProArt' group were repeatedly discussed in the weekly staff meetings – but this achieved nothing. Whereas before the parties had consisted only of a few committed people (the majority of the other teachers had stayed on

the mechanics were professionally behind the times, incompetent, sloppy and generally unable to learn. The most authoritarian of the mechanics, he said, had appointed himself as a spokesman for the team and was continually fuelling the conflict. His motives were well known, he said: he had not been able to get over his severe disappointment at not being promoted to team leader. The team members, on the other hand, agreed that the only reason their team leader insisted on his superior position was that he lacked factual arguments. They felt that, as a young engineer, he lacked practical experience and could not tolerate older and more experienced colleagues. In informal conversations they described their boss as opinionated and unforgiving, not quite up to the demands of his job. They made a written complaint about their boss to the factory management, which was met with a harsh rebuke from the plant manager. Other managers in the plant also made no secret of the fact that they condemned 'such unfair attacks' against a line manager and that they supported the maintenance team leader. The mechanics went to the trade union for advice.

the sidelines), the groups were now enlisting supporters. The 'Progressives' publicized their view that the 'ProArt' people had very little experience of the real world, that they shied away from facing harsh realities and were trying to overprotect the young people. They said that the curriculum had become unbalanced, and that more and more parents had taken their children out of the school. This had created financial difficulties for the school. The key members of the 'ProArt' group were questioning the pedagogical knowledge of the key members of the 'Progressives': they had only superficial knowledge of the basics of alternative education, were too lenient towards the young people, going as far as pandering to them, were undermining recognized school rules etc. It was time, they said, for the head teacher to start disciplinary proceedings. Some pupils, as well as parents, took sides with one or the other party. Once the parents had found out about the conflict as well, some removed their children from the school. There were rumours within the school that some of the most popular young teachers wanted to leave the school.

Each conflict party creates a positive image of its own side, a negative one of the other side, for example:[6]

- I know a lot but ...
- My knowledge is always up to date but ...
- I am a good learner but ...

- I am accurate but ...

- etc.

- The other side knows little
- The other side's knowledge is hopelessly out of date
- The other side is unable to learn
- The other side is inaccurate ...
- etc.

One thing is important: on level 4 the enemy image consists of judgements about the knowledge and abilities of the opposing party. Moral judgements are still consciously avoided. If they do creep in, they are quickly corrected.

Self-image and enemy image are firmly fixed in people's consciousness and are no longer corrected even if differing (objectively ascertainable) facts emerge in encounters with the opponent. On the contrary, the existing judgement about the enemy appears to be continuously reaffirmed by new experiences. This is because people's perceptiveness is already severely restricted. They only see what conforms to their own judgement. This is the psychological mechanism of the 'self-fulfilling prophecy', i.e. the conflict parties do not see that, through the fixed image they have of each other, they are manoeuvring each other into the extreme positions that they are in fact fighting against. In the school example this means that the more authoritarian the 'Progressives' perceive the head teacher's actions to be, the more their behaviour – mostly subconscious – challenges the head teacher to show her authoritarian side. And this is exactly what they are fighting against. They provoke each other through many small snide remarks in order to increase their contempt for the opposing party; but they try to do it in such a way that there is no proof that they are trying to be provocative.

This behaviour shows the mechanisms described[7] as 'paradoxical relationships' and 'double binds': the team leader wants the team spokesman to be the villain so that he can 'beat him up'; yet subconsciously he does everything he can to keep the spokesman in the organization because he still needs him as a lightning conductor to defuse his own stresses. Accusations are used to create guilt in the other party, and this guilt ties the parties to each other until the scores are finally settled.

Prejudice largely arises by means of the psychological mechanism of projection: one party mainly sees the annoying characteristics of the opposing party; they get annoyed about those characteristics because subconsciously they know that they themselves have them as well. They notice the mote in the eye of the opposing party, but not the beam that is in their own.

Key members of the group try to involve other people in the conflict and to enlist supporters. This is done by bringing up the stereotypical image of the enemy in conversation. When somebody agrees with this image, they are halfway to becoming a supporter.

5.5 Escalation level 5: loss of face

On level 4 accusations about shortcomings in the other side's knowledge and abilities, and their irritating behaviour, were at the core of the enemy image. Various circumstances suddenly lead a party to believe that they can see the real, reprehensible intentions of the enemy. Hurtful remarks and insults are no longer accidental but become intentional. The disagreement has abruptly become radical and brutal – verbally, and perhaps even physically.

The team leader began to suspect that the mechanics wanted to undermine his new managerial position within the company; he thought that this was why they were trying to bring about the failure of his new maintenance system. As a precautionary measure he began to draw up a so-called 'black book', i.e. he kept

During a parents' evening concerned parents wanted to know to what extent rumours were to be believed that some teachers were to be dismissed because of the school's financial difficulties. The head teacher had been evasive and had said that the school was in a period of transition and that pedagogical questions had to be

exact records about the jobs allocated and their implement-ation, as well as any machine breakdowns. In addition he asked production staff what they thought of the individual mechanics' professional abilities. Through this questioning his suspicions of the team spokesperson hardened: he thought that this person was sabotaging the new system as an act of revenge for the fact that he had not been promoted to team leader himself.

During a meeting of the 'customer focus' project team the team leader surprised the spokes-man by presenting a number of figures and accused him of deliberately damaging the company. Completely taken by surprise, the spokesman could not come up with any convincing answers, got caught up in contradictions and in turn raised massive accusations against his boss. The team leader then accused the spokesman of lying and suspended him with immediate effect. Legal steps were to follow.

News of these events spread through the company like wildfire and led people to side passionately with one or the other party.

reconsidered. In fact, she said, urgently required savings were being explored, but redundancies were not on the agenda.

In the next staff meeting the spokesman of the 'Progressives' picked up on these remarks by the head teacher and accused her of manipulation. He said that during a conversation with well-informed parents he had been shown a highly confidential list of teachers whose dismissal the head teacher was proposing to the governors. When the head teacher responded with confusion, the spokesman of the 'Progressives' presented her with a copy of the 'redundancies' list which was signed by the head teacher. Seven of the eight people named belonged to the 'Pro-gressives'. This revelation caused great consternation. The core group of the 'Progressives' declared that they 'were withdrawing their confidence from the manipulative head teacher' and demanded that she leave the meeting immediately. Some people joined the 'Pro-gressives', others defended the head teacher. She left the room in tears, and her deputy closed the tumultuous meeting.

The threshold to level 5 is very dramatic. It is crossed when, in a blinding realization, one conflict party thinks that it finally sees the true, destructive intentions of the enemy: 'The head teacher is not a poor chair. She deliberately creates chaos so that she can manipulate people more easily!' Belief in the moral integrity of the enemy has been lost. This is a dis-illusioning experience because people are suddenly able to see through the 'illusion' of before. The previously perceived negative characteristics of the enemy turn out to be much worse. The enemy is seen as having only dangerous and morally corrupt characteristics of the Shadow personality, the *Negative Double*. The other side's Light personality, the ideals and Higher Self it might harbour, are no longer perceived.[8] An angel confronts a devil: each side's self-image is heightened and appears more virtuous than it actually is; the enemy image takes on extreme proportions – even becoming animalistic and diabolical.

This disillusioning revelation also leads each side to see previous encounters with the diabolical enemy in a different light. In retrospect different experiences are interpreted in such a way that the enemy's corruption was seen to be at work even then.

When one conflict party experiences the other in this way, it ruthlessly goes on the offensive, passionately looking for ways and means and 'degrading rituals'[9] in order to attack the opposing party's façade ruthlessly and directly, and to 'unmask' it, i.e. to expose its true nature. The attackers see it as their 'sacred duty' to open the eyes of others as well, and to prove how corrupt the basic nature of the opponent really is. People think that they cannot co-operate with the personification of evil, immorality, pathological and criminal behaviour! This step in the escalation of a conflict is always evidenced by radical, ruthless language,[10] as if people were no longer dealing with other human beings: 'The enemy must be wiped out, kicked out, eliminated ...'

The party that is being attacked fights back, publicly loses face through being exposed and becomes an outcast. From now on it is isolated, avoided and boycotted – as are other people who continue to be sympathetic. This also means that the outcasts are cut off from an exchange of feedback which could allow them to modify their own behaviour in response.[11]

Each outcast party usually sees itself as a scapegoat as well, blamed for various problems within the organization. It can't recognize itself in the diabolical image and feels completely misunderstood and treated unfairly. Therefore it is very likely to consider a counterattack, which in turn is intended to lead to a loss of face for the other party. The side bemoans its fate and only listens to the voices of those who confirm its outrage over the fate it has suffered. And it stubbornly seeks to rehabilitate its good reputation at any price! The search to reclaim its lost honour can be conducted with great passion, even obsessively.

All these events severely shake the self-image of the key people and of the group as a whole, leading to profound erosion of the group. The group that is pushing the other one out often harbours the illusion that, if only the villain disappears, normal life could be resumed. But a conflict which has escalated this far causes problems in many areas and changes the whole group: it will never go back to the way it was before ...

At this point I want to emphasize a difference in terminology: in general usage, 'loss of face' is sometimes used to refer to a person who, for example, has lost a directorship as part of a reorganization and is now only a departmental manager; or it is used to describe a loss of certain status symbols (company car, large office). In these cases, loss of face would only describe a loss of status, prestige or similar. This is not what is meant here. In the language of conflict psychology[12] loss of face is much more dramatic and always means that the moral identity of a person is destroyed. When somebody has 'lost face', they have lost their moral credibility.

5.6 Escalation level 6: strategies of threat

When, after all this, it has still not been possible to find a way out of the conflict, the escalation continues with particular intensity, as shown by the two practical examples.

The personnel department issued a warning to the team of mechanics and prepared to dismiss the team's spokesman. Meetings of the maintenance team were suspended until further notice. In the meantime the spokesman had been barred from entering the factory and he was therefore consulting a legal adviser from the union and secretly meeting with his team mates in order to discuss the way forward.

In order to put the company under moral pressure he telephoned to threaten that he would pass on concrete evidence to the press about severe criminal violations of environmental legislation on the part of the factory management. These violations had been covered up by the company at the time. As the management refuted these allegations, the local press ran some articles which blamed the company for smaller environmental violations and which demanded that environmental agencies and/or the courts should intervene.

Events snowballed from now on. The head teacher denied that she had seriously considered redundancies and went off sick for several days. During this time she had several confidential discussions with the governors, who had in fact been in charge of new appointments and dismissals previously. The governing body split into two factions, for and against the head teacher. In the next staff meeting the 'Progressives' presented additional incriminating evidence and intensified their demands for suspending the head teacher. When the governors rejected this, some parents threatened to inform the tax office about unlawful payments to the head teacher and to several teachers – and this would lead to criminal action by the tax authorities. In response the chair and treasurer of the governing body were deeply hurt and resigned. The remaining officers now threatened to dismiss the 'Progressives' after all because their behaviour had brought the school into serious disrepute.

The parties present their demands and want to force each other to give in. In order to get a demand (1) met, a punishment (2 – negative sanction), a damaging consequence, is announced; and in order to ensure that the opponent takes all this seriously, the party has to show that they are actually able to go through with the punishment (3 – sanction potential). These three factors are the corner points of the triangle of threats (Figure 5.2):

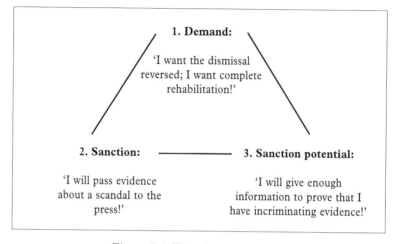

Figure 5.2: The triangle of threats

Only the party that is threatened can decide whether to take the threat seriously, or whether to dismiss it as mere sabre-rattling. The threatening side therefore tries to ensure that the demand bears a credible correlation to the damage that is threatened: a substantial demand ([1] e.g '10 million pounds ransom, ...') in conjunction with great potential damage ([2] e.g. '... otherwise a building will be blown up!') is credible; if one is too serious and the other too weak, or vice versa, there is a lack of credibility. The party must also be able to show that it has the required detonators and that it is truly prepared to go as far as it claims. This works best when implementation of the sanction can begin in small doses.

Threats are generally met with counter-threats. Decisions are governed by 'pessimistic anticipation' (Chapter 3). Ultimatum and counter-ultimatum also increase the pressure of time: decisions have to be made quickly, actions need to be incisive! By increasing the pressure on the enemy, each side becomes publicly associated with the threat and its consequences, locking itself into a compulsion to act and losing the initiative: it has to react rather than act. Thus neither party can retreat without losing its credibility at this juncture.[13]

The threat and the potential danger arising from it have ever greater consequences, and more parties are drawn into the conflict. Things can become critical for the people and groups around the conflict parties. As the conflict causes ever greater ripples, it becomes more difficult to contain it. As the threatener and the threatened increasingly act under stress, they tend to overreact, and this causes more unintended side effects than intended main effects.

5.7 Escalation level 7: limited destructive blows

At this point it should be said that the case studies used so far are, as has already been stated, a mixture of several similar cases from my professional experience. In reality I was called in as an external adviser at around the beginning of level 6 and I was able to work towards a constructive solution to the conflict. The conflict did not escalate further from this point. In the following sections I therefore present events which, within the dynamics of the conflict, might have been possible. I am doing this so that the reader can get a clear idea of the next steps in the escalation in the same organizational context of the factory and the school. Therefore I have fictitiously shifted actual events from conflict escalation in other organizations into these two organizations, as if they had actually happened in the case studies described so far. So for levels 7, 8 and 9 I should say:

This is how – considering everything that happened before – the conflict might have continued to escalate:

The team spokesman is dismissed with immediate effect and instigates proceedings against his dismissal. The environmental

The events lead to the formation of factions in various different forums. The head teacher insists she is innocent and demands harsh measures

agencies, political parties and interest groups become involved in the matter. One night a cupboard in the office of the company's director is forced open and many documents disappear. Investigations bring to light further evidence for environmental offences that had been covered up. The authorities receive copies of incriminating documents from an anonymous informer. This leads to criminal proceedings against the company management. One production unit has to be temporarily suspended. The dismissed team spokesman is publicly accused of having organized the break-in. An anonymous letter is sent to other companies in the area, warning them against employing the obstinate mechanic.

against the 'destructive elements'. People are looking everywhere to find traitors and apportion blame for the situation. The governing body has to take over the day-to-day running of the school and is overstretched because they have to deal with many personnel matters and financial salvage actions. The tax office is tipped off and carries out a detailed examination of the school's financial affairs. Mistakes are uncovered, and these are prosecuted as tax evasion. Evidence is found that the head teacher misinformed the governing body and teachers. A key member of the 'Progressives' is accused and prosecuted for passing on drugs to children, another is accused of attempted sexual abuse of young people.

Threats are implemented. The conflict parties only treat each other as 'inanimate objects'. They have lost their belief in the opponent's humanity. First they destroy only objects which might have been used to bring about the sanctions attached to the threat; later people are included in the destruction.

The fighting parties are quite clear that there are no longer any victories to be won. The decisive factor is whether the loss to the opposing side is greater than its own damage – this is then (re)defined as a 'benefit'. Damage becomes joy, becomes gloating. The enemy is forced to make involuntary sacrifices – extracted through destruction.

Deceit and lies become the greatest virtues in war, finally turning central moral values into their opposites.

5.8 Escalation level 8: fragmentation of the enemy

If the damage on level 7 remained fairly limited, the stakes are now raised with each blow and counterblow. Once the threshold to level 8 is crossed, the conflict becomes an 'all or nothing' fight: the enemy is to be destroyed – materially and/or psychologically and/or spiritually.

Customers, suppliers, banks etc. receive anonymous letters with information about the scandals within the company; as a result they increasingly pull away from 'Boilerworks'. Good managers and specialist staff leave the company. The production quality drops dramatically, costs rise. The company management feels forced to close down operations. The dismissed team spokesman is totally boycotted within the area, his wife treated like an outcast within the town. Even his grown-up children increasingly have difficulties at their workplaces and are eventually left with only one option: to move to a different part of the country and seek alternative employment.

The schools inspector, having waited for a considerable period, finally intervenes and forces the governing body to resign. The head teacher and a substantial number of teachers are removed from the school; some are barred from continuing in their profession. A large number of pupils move to another school. The parents of the pupils in the top form who had failed to pass their final examinations sue the school for damages. Many parents who had given the school interest-free loans for improvement works withdraw their funds, triggering financial catastrophe. The school has to declare bankruptcy.

The vital organs of the opponents' system are attacked and paralysed. Today it is enough to focus destructive efforts on a company's computer systems to bring about a breakdown of the system. All that is required to break down an organization through its own centrifugal tendency would be to disrupt, for example, some of its management systems: quality control, financial control, sales ledger, time records, attendance control etc.

The opposing party is broken up by deliberately and purposefully weakening its internal cohesion and paralysing important functions. Eventually it disintegrates – psychologically, spiritually or physically – to such an extent that it cannot rebuild itself.

5.9 Escalation level 9: together into the abyss

The opposing parties can see no way back. Total confrontation is aimed at complete destruction of the opponent. It is enough for one party to be prepared to go to extremes, without restraint, and not to shy away from totally destructive measures, even if this leads to self-destruction. When the conflict has crossed the threshold to escalation level 9, even self-destruction can be experienced as a triumph insofar as the opponent is also pulled down into the abyss.

This is what the bitter end in the factory and the school might have looked like:

The former team spokesman wages a bitter legal battle against 'Boiler-works', going through all the courts. He loses the rest of his money and gets into horrendous debts. The highest court also finds against him, and his house has to be auctioned off …

The key players take each other to court, and there is physical violence between the people involved. This leads to criminal proceedings. In one case the violence even leads to a suicide.

However, life can write even crueller tragedies than fiction.

5.10 What powers are at work in the escalation of conflict?

Figure 5.3 shows the main characteristics of the nine levels of escalation that can occur in conflicts between two people, in groups, or between groups and organizations.

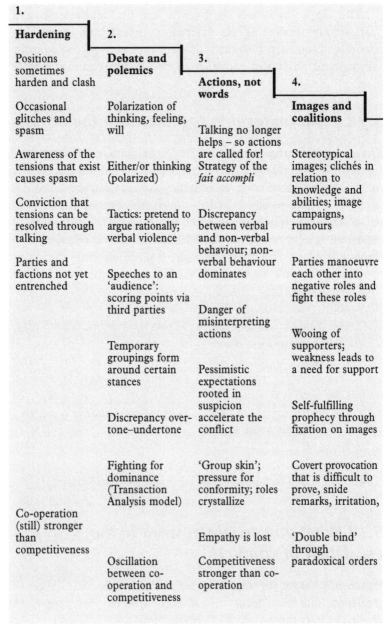

1. **Hardening**	**2.** **Debate and polemics**	**3.** **Actions, not words**	**4.** **Images and coalitions**
Positions sometimes harden and clash	Polarization of thinking, feeling, will	Talking no longer helps – so actions are called for! Strategy of the *fait accompli*	Stereotypical images; clichés in relation to knowledge and abilities; image campaigns, rumours
Occasional glitches and spasm			
Awareness of the tensions that exist causes spasm	Either/or thinking (polarized)		
Conviction that tensions can be resolved through talking	Tactics: pretend to argue rationally; verbal violence	Discrepancy between verbal and non-verbal behaviour; non-verbal behaviour dominates	
Parties and factions not yet entrenched	Speeches to an 'audience': scoring points via third parties	Danger of misinterpreting actions	Parties manoeuvre each other into negative roles and fight these roles
	Temporary groupings form around certain stances	Pessimistic expectations rooted in suspicion accelerate the conflict	Wooing of supporters; weakness leads to a need for support
	Discrepancy overtone–undertone		Self-fulfilling prophecy through fixation on images
	Fighting for dominance (Transaction Analysis model)	'Group skin'; pressure for conformity; roles crystallize	Covert provocation that is difficult to prove, snide remarks, irritation,
Co-operation (still) stronger than competitiveness		Empathy is lost	'Double bind' through paradoxical orders
	Oscillation between co-operation and competitiveness	Competitiveness stronger than co-operation	

Figure 5.3: Overview of the nine levels of escalation

5. Loss of face	6. Strategies of threat	7. Limited destructive blows	8. Fragment-ation of the enemy	9. Together into the abyss
Public and direct personal attacks – moral integrity is lost	Spiral of threats and counter-threats:	Thinking only revolves around 'inanimate objects'	Bringing about total breakdown of the enemy system	No way back
Staging of unmasking activities as a ritual: exposure leads to dis-illusionment; works retro-spectively	Triangle of threats: correlation demand/punish-ment/potential for punishment; credibility through proportionality	Human qualities no longer valid	Destroying vital system factors to make the system unmanageable	Total confrontation
Image: angel–devil, Double	Locking in oneself and each other ('trip wires')	Limited destruction as 'appropriate response' (avoidance of excessive counterblows)	Isolating 'front fighters from their hinterland'	Destruction of the enemy even at the price of self-destruction
Disgust, casting out, banishing	Manoeuvring oneself into compulsion to act; loss of initiative	Reversal of values and virtues into their oppo-sites: relatively small damage is considered a 'benefit'	Complete destruction: body, soul and spirit	Enjoyment of self-destruction – provided the enemy will not survive!
Loss of external perceptivenes; isolation in the 'echo cave'	Stress increased through ultimatums and counter-ultimatums; scissor effect			Willingness to cause severe damage to the environment or successors through one's own downfall
Ideology, values, principles!	Acceleration			
Striving for rehabilitation				

This description of the dynamics of escalation could give the impression that, as human beings, we are powerless and at the mercy of superior powers which inevitably draw us from level 1 to the abyss of level 9. And mighty powers are, in fact, at work as the conflict escalates. But we are not at their mercy without any powers of our own. At each threshold we are basically able to 'wake up', become aware of what is happening and put an end to our actions. Conflicts only continue to escalate if we allow this to happen. The destruction only takes on ever-greater dimensions if we ignore the signals of our awareness at the different thresholds and if we allow ourselves to be pulled along on the tide of our powerful drives and passions.

In our subconscious we have a negative potential which enables us to carry out terrible and inhuman actions. The history books are full of evidence of those fatal basic instincts. Through carelessness and clouding of our awareness – initially only minor – we allow certain powers of our subconscious to surface. We provoke and mobilize them in each other, unleash them, and later it becomes very hard to keep them under control. Once we have allowed them to enter the arena of the conflict, they have the potential to pull us down with them. In conflict situations people descend to the deepest regions of the inferno, of the underworld, as often described in epics such as Dante's *Divine Comedy* or in myths and fables.

Against the background of this archetypal image I always describe the escalation as a downward movement, into the underworld and baser nature of individual people and groups. As the escalation progresses, the link with the Light personality (Chapter 2) is increasingly lost. Each action provokes negative powers in the subconscious of the opposing party. Reactions occur which are no longer controlled by the Ego or the Higher Self. Therefore the way out of escalation is always a confrontation with one's own alien, darker sides. The following chapters are designed to provide help with this.

6. What can I do as soon as I notice a conflict?

Chapters 4 and 5 have shown that conflicts don't usually come as a big surprise, let alone begin with a loud fanfare. Instead, minor frictions and tensions gradually progress in small stages until they become serious conflicts. Therefore people should, as often as possible, try to practise recognizing first minor signals. There are more than enough opportunities to practise, as newspapers and the specialist press regularly carry reports about conflicts. Reading and analysing such stories is a good opportunity. The following exercise (Figure 6.1) helps with practising assessment of the dynamics of escalation through newspaper articles.

Carefully read a newspaper report about conflict at least twice before proceeding with the analysis and answering the following questions:

1. Which main characteristics are directly recognizable? What clear indicators are there?
2. On which points am I unsure? On which aspects do I have to make assumptions? Clearly articulate your assumptions and make notes.
3. Check the description of the situation once more: what supports your assumptions, what speaks against them? You will then notice other symptoms as well. If you still can't find clear indicators for certain assumptions, follow the stories in the next editions of the newspaper.
4. Try to make a prognosis: how might the conflict continue? Which alternatives are likely to be apparent to the people involved in the situation? What are the potential consequences of the continuation of the conflict as you see it develop?

> 5. Continue to follow the story. Check your assumptions and prognoses. If you have to correct your prognosis, check which symptoms you might have overlooked, underestimated, misinterpreted.

Figure 6.1: Exercise to assess the level of escalation

You can improve the accuracy of your assessment by doing this and similar exercises. As soon as you become uncertain, you have to look again at the dynamics of the conflict and the characteristics of the escalation levels. This book has only been able to describe the main features. If you are still unclear about the terminology used, I would recommend that you read the full description in my book on conflict management[1] (only available in German), as a simplified description like the one included here cannot do full justice to the reality of conflict.

You can only begin to tackle the differences that have emerged with any prospect of success if you have correctly identified the level of escalation. However, there is another danger here: even if you are good at recognizing and differentiating the levels of escalation, you might still argue about this with your conflict partners. I showed in Chapter 1 (see Figure 1.12 and Figure 1.13) how the 'self-infection mechanisms' of conflicts can add personal differences to the factual differences of opinion; and these can lead to conflict about the conflict. It is very likely that the different people involved in the conflict will perceive the escalation level they are currently at in slightly different ways. Therefore, if you want to discuss the conflict with the opposing party, this will cause additional tensions. 'Conflict about the conflict' then results, through the mechanism of self-infection. This often leads to the conflict trap, whereby one party thinks the other one deliberately and dishonestly misrepresents things and events, and the argument will become a 'conflict about the conflict resolution'. But if each party reads and discusses the characteristics of the escalation levels described in this book, they are better able to discuss their assessment of how far the conflict has escalated.

The following figure (6.2) summarizes the content of Figures 1.12 and 1.13 in one diagram and shows the limits of self-help.

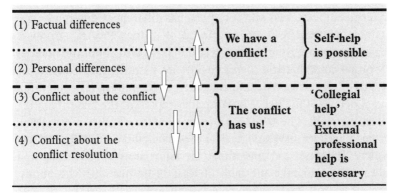

*Figure 6.2: 'Self-infection' in conflict situations,
and the limits of self-help*

The examples given in Chapters 4 and 5 show how 'self-infection' followed by escalation can occur during the course of a difference of opinion. The example of the Erasmus School first centres on factual differences (1): a group of teachers wants to extend IT teaching in order to prepare children for the demands of professional life; the other group considers extending art lessons more useful.

During the disagreement the relationships between the participants begin to suffer (2): both sides are annoyed about the perceived intransigence and unreasonable behaviour of the opposing side. Therefore differences in the interpersonal area have been added to factual differences. However, these personal differences in turn affect existing differences of opinion on factual matters: the participants want to present their stances more clearly. Therefore they formulate their different opinions or aims more forcibly than before and the positions begin to polarize. Yet this intensifies the existing anger on each side even further, as each side thinks 'We're not stupid – we only assess the importance of art lessons differently! So don't be so arrogant; you should be more receptive and listen to our reasonable arguments!'

After several disagreements there is infection on the next level (3): 'conflict about the conflict' emerges. This is because, as a result of the communication problems which occurred, each side interprets the factual and interpersonal differences differently: the young 'Progressives' are convinced that the 'ProArt' group is basically remote from the real world, has no idea about the realities of professional life and therefore pursues a strategy of isolation; the young 'Progressives' believe that their older colleagues prevent an open debate of the issues because they represent the majority of the teaching staff. The 'ProArt' faction sees the conflict as resulting from a lack of psychological and pedagogical knowledge of the young 'Progressives'; they think the latter are too superficial and always want to take the path of least resistance with the pupils; therefore they keep trying to form alliances with certain parents and pupils. As a result both parties articulate their arguments more forcefully than previously.

As the differences increase rather than reduce, both parties are thinking about possible solutions. But as they perceive the reasons for and background to the conflict differently, they come up with different proposals to resolve the conflict. These proposals are then rejected by the other side, creating a further level of differences: (4) 'conflict about the conflict resolution'. And, because of disagreement about ways to resolve the conflict, differences in perception of the reasons for and background to the conflict on level (3) deepen; these stronger contrasts in turn affect the interpersonal level (2) and intensify the factual differences (1). The game can then continue with the next cycle of self-infection.

Many organizations are in a state of 'conflict about the conflict resolution' by the time somebody suggests that external advice should be sought. The conflict parties will have tried in vain to resolve the differences themselves. But as the self-infection has already reached deeper levels, all well-meaning attempts to resolve the situation have only resulted in further poisoning. The conflict about conflict resolution makes things even more complicated than it was. Therefore the conflict will continue to escalate even if each party individually makes serious efforts to do something to resolve it. Tragically, the effect is the opposite of what was intended.

All this can cause a failure of attempts to tackle the first weak signals. Figure 6.2 shows how the four levels of entanglement limit the potential of self-help. Even if the conflict parties themselves are well-trained conflict experts or mediators, they will rarely be able to bring about positive results through their own efforts. This is because they no longer believe in each other's objectivity. Therefore I would urgently recommend enlisting outside help.

It is most likely that the participants in the conflict will always perceive events differently: after all, subjective and distorted differences in perception are typical for the dynamics of all conflicts. Therefore different ('asymmetrical') assessments of the level of conflict may occur throughout the process of escalation. However, in my experience the perceptions and assessments of the present escalation level hardly ever deviate by more than two escalation levels. The explanation is quite simple: after a while the behaviour of the party experiencing the lower escalation level pulls the opposing party down with it, thus creating the reality it subjectively perceived.

6.1 Unilaterally articulating 'I-messages'

When you notice first signals, it is advisable to talk to the other party about the perceived frictions and tensions. But in order to avoid conflict about the conflict, the tensions are best discussed in the form of *'I-messages'*, never as so-called 'you-messages'. I-messages are very important as **I** use them to express what **I** feel, what moves **me**, how **I** feel physically and so on. The purpose is not to condemn or change behaviour or characteristics of my counterpart, as this almost always results in a *turning away*, i.e. rejection or annoyance. Instead, I-messages are intended to be a statement of facts without simultaneously devaluing the recipient of the message or placing him under pressure to justify himself or to act. I-messages are also intended to express a joint responsibility of the speaker in the situation that has arisen, and to cause the other party to *turn towards* the situation by thinking about and being interested in it. If I articulate an I-message correctly, my counterpart will hear directly from me something he could otherwise only deduce or speculate about from my tone of voice, my facial expression and my body language.

Therefore giving I-messages needs to be thoroughly practised in order to avoid problems at the very beginning, and to prevent them from simply being 'you-messages' in disguise.[1] Here is an exercise:

Think of a specific interpersonal encounter that you felt did not go well. First recall this situation in all its details:

1. Ask yourself: What did I feel? Which signals did my body give me? How and where did I perceive these?
2. Articulate your sensations or emotions, always starting sentences with 'I felt ..., I experienced ...' etc.
   Correct I-messages might be statements such as *I didn't feel quite right. I sensed tension in my stomach. I felt insecure...*
   Watch out: The following statements aren't I-messages; they are *you-messages in disguise:*
   '**You** made me feel bad. **You** made me feel tense. **You** made me feel insecure.' These statements don't express **my** feelings; they are an accusation or a demand presented to my counterpart.
3. Practise pure I-messages in different situations, taking care that no you-messages are hidden in them.
   The important checks are as follows: Might my counterpart feel criticized by my statement? Or feel that I am asking him to act against his convictions? Or am I interpreting his intentions in you-messages?
4. Consciously practise giving *you-messages* in the same situations. How are they different?
   Imagine what your counterpart might feel or think on hearing this message.
5. Imagine how your counterpart might articulate his own *I-messages:* 'In these situations these messages might go something like this: ....'
6. What feelings do you think these formulations might trigger for you? Again, articulate the emotions you are likely to have using I-messages.
7. How would you feel if your counterpart addressed you using *you-messages?*
   Articulate your reaction: 'I think I might feel ...'
8. Summarize what you have learned as if you had to explain to another person what is important for giving I-messages correctly.

Figure 6.3: Practising I-messages.[2]

Correctly formulated I-messages don't make any demands; they only let your counterpart know what you feel or what you are worried about. At most you might invite your partners to express an I-message of their own: 'How did you feel at that time? What was that like for you?' I-messages generally create interest and mutual opening up, as they do not violate the freedom and autonomy of the other person. If you articulate your worries without making any accusations, you can communicate and share your concerns. Your concerns and the concerns of your counterpart can become something you share, creating a good basis for mutually supportive action.

If your opponent does not as yet experience the situation as problematic, he might show an interest in your perception and you can share with him the tensions you perceive. You just need to be careful not to try to persuade your counterpart to come over to your viewpoint. Perhaps certain events worried you more than they did your partner? By using I-messages and through talking you might be able to get the other person interested in reading the description of the escalation levels at his leisure. You might also be able to have a conversation about this when the opportunity arises. As long as the conflict hasn't escalated beyond level 2 or 3, this approach will still be fairly easy.

6.2 Articulating the unwanted, 'non-values'

The next technique can also be very useful for articulating tensions at an early stage. 'Non-values'[3] means that a certain course of events is not wanted, that it is of no value to me and that I therefore try not to let things get that far. By articulating my non-values I tell the opposing party that I want to set limits for myself because I **do** care which way the conflict goes. For example, a Boilerworks mechanic might say to his boss: 'I definitely don't want production to be affected by our differences about the maintenance system. And I definitely don't want us to lose customers because of this.'

This method can be very useful up to escalation level 7, although it is advisable to enlist a neutral person or body to seek a resolution in a conflict that has escalated this far.

In my experience this method has very direct and powerful effects because:

- Generally, I am showing that I want to limit damaging effects;
- I am bringing up potential effects which my opponent might have assumed to be intentional – and thus defusing any fearful fantasies;
- I am showing that I feel responsible for my actions and omissions, that I want to avoid a compulsive interlocking of action and reaction;
- I am not apportioning blame;
- Finally, my statement might invite the opposing party to indicate that somehow he himself is not entirely happy with the way things have gone so far.

The 'non-values' technique can be practised according to the following guidelines:

The example of the 'Erasmus School' conflict shows how 'non-values', what is unwanted, might be articulated:

1. I imagine where the situation that has emerged might *drift* if we don't take constructive steps in time: 'The parents will lose confidence in our competence as teachers: they will remove the children from our school. The financial contributions of the parents are drastically reduced; colleagues will have to be dismissed ...'
2. I imagine what things might look like in the school in about six months' time if the situation continues in this way, with all the accompanying *emotions:* 'I would blame myself for having watched events unfold without doing anything. I would feel powerless. I would be angry with my own group, because we have allowed ourselves to be carried away like this ...'
3. I articulate clearly the situation that would be undesirable for me: 'I don't want the atmosphere amongst the staff to get any worse. I don't want one of you or one of us to become ill. I wouldn't like it if our school's reputation were to suffer ...'

---

4. I express where I feel personal responsibility in the situation: 'I don't want to end up blaming myself for not trying harder. I feel personally responsible for contributing to openness in our communication ...'

5. I can say to my counterpart: 'I'd like to know what concerns the situation that has emerged triggers for you!' Here, too, I need to be very careful not to express any expectations about the other person's behaviour.

6. I look back on the experience of doing this exercise and summarize my conclusions as a briefing for a colleague or other partner.

Figure 6.4: Articulating 'non-values'

As with the I-messages, it is important not to include any hidden criticisms of the opponent's behaviour when making statements about 'non-values'.

I-messages or 'non-values' statements are easier if you practise keeping in mind your feelings and staying in touch with them. If you can't hold a dialogue with your own feelings, you will be unable to communicate with other people about theirs.

6.3 Talking about emerging conflicts in a group

All the methods described so far can be used to begin to clarify one-to-one relationships. In groups many people find it harder to begin the process of tackling conflict. The dangers that have been highlighted multiply in groups because there is a clash not just of two different viewpoints and sets of interests but of several people's.

The following pointers are not intended as a panacea, but to illustrate behavioural principles in group situations. This is because the main principles which apply in group work are similar to those for working on one-to-one relationships: both situations hinge on an awareness of different perceptions and viewpoints; in both cases I-messages are important; and in both situations it is beneficial to articulate 'non-values' and to see whether agreement can be reached over what would be undesirable. Consensus about non-values forms a good basis for reaching consensus about positive values at a later point.

Once you have decided to raise a problem that worries you in a group, then I-messages are the most useful. Describe your impressions, your emotions and invite the others to talk about their feelings, hopes and fears. It is good to show people your own feelings of insecurity, worry etc. in this situation, not trying to pretend that you feel superior. Being honest about one's feeling is the secret of success. Steiner[4] once used the following fitting description in a public speaking course: 'It really is true that nobody is interested in our thoughts as such, that everyone is annoyed by another person's intentions and that the impression, the effect (...) of a speech depends solely on our feelings.'

Moreover, it is important to emphasize that you are, of course, expressing your own personal and subjective perceptions and feelings. You are not trying to pronounce eternal truths, you are conscious that your viewpoint is relative. Therefore it is also necessary to compare your viewpoint with the perception of other people. You can also say that you consider a completely different view of things just as valid. If, by doing this, you show an interest in other ways of seeing things, then there is no need to argue over whether or not you have a one-sided view of the situation.

When raising the problems you perceive, the so-called 'prolepsis' technique can also defuse the situation. This Greek word means 'anticipating a potential counter-argument'. This technique is often used in court trials: before the partner or opponent raises an objection, you have already done so and begun to discuss it. Prolepsis statements often begin 'At this point you might say that ...' And in the next statement the valid objection is presented seriously and in detail. This clearly shows respect for different viewpoints, demonstrating the fact that the other opinion is valued – it is the opposite of disregarding or devaluing different viewpoints.

Finally, it is also most useful to explain what you **don't want to achieve** (non-values) with your statements in the following way: 'I don't want to dramatize the situation to exert pressure or frighten people. I don't think that fear is beneficial, and pressure only provokes counter-pressure. I am simply concerned to see how ...'

In some groups it is very difficult for people to articulate freely their feelings and subjective viewpoints. Perhaps talking about emotions is even a taboo? If this is the case, the so-called 'rotating diary'[5] might be a very simple but effective method. To do this, participants agree in advance that the discussion will be interrupted briefly after 15 minutes. Each person has a sheet of paper and draws a vertical line all the way down the middle of their sheet. In the break each person writes down a maximum of three lines in the left-hand column about what he thought, felt and wanted in the previous session. In the right-hand column he writes down what he is hoping for, or what his fears are, for the coming session. Then each person hands the sheet to his neighbour on the right and probably reads what he received from the left. After another 15 minutes each person writes on the sheet he received from the left: again, on the left, what he thought, felt and wanted during the preceding session; and on the right what he fears and hopes for from the coming round. After several rounds all participants read out what is written on the last sheet they received.

This is one of many careful ways of awakening interest for problems that exist. However, not every group is as fearful of confrontation as I assumed just now. If not, then indicators of irritations and tensions may be welcomed and supported. For example, one team member might offer to lead a 'public interview' in front of the whole group, first with a representative of one party, then with one from the other. The interviewer asks detailed questions on the way people see things; whether they can imagine how the other side might experience the situation etc. As it is a public interview with the whole team present, one side immediately finds out what the other side thinks, feels and wants, and how it has perceived the events. Yet the interview is conducted 'privately', as if the other side weren't present. When the two main representatives have been interviewed, it would be advisable to give the other team members a chance to speak as well.

Once the first signals of conflict are acknowledged, the group can nominate several people to a 'preparation team' (often called 'confidential circle', 'discussion committee', 'ombudsman' or similar). This group considers how it might continue working on the conflict. The forum in which signals can be given to point out the existence of conflict is not necessarily the best forum for working on the conflict. It is important to ensure that every forum allows the signalling of problems; if there is any restriction on this, emergency signals would inevitably be suppressed. However, careful consideration is needed to decide where, how and by whom conflicts are worked on.

As has already been mentioned, the examples given above are not meant to be copied exactly; they are the basic elements of an approach. These elements must be weighted differently in each specific situation, and each person will use them differently.

It would, of course, be ideal, if a group has an annual 'stock-taking' session on problems and conflicts. Some organizations not only produce an annual balance sheet and profit-and-loss account, they also carry out an annual evaluation of the working atmosphere, of people's job satisfaction and of indicators of tensions and con-flicts. In healthcare it has already been proven that preventive medicine costs less than curative medicine – and that the former allows people to live healthier and happier lives. The same goes for organizations. If they are conflict-resistant – as described in Chapter 1 – they will be better able to meet the challenges of the future.

6.4 Self-help is followed by collegial help or professional advice

The methods shown here can be used as self-help techniques provided the conflict hasn't escalated beyond level 3. As shown in Chapter 1, this is roughly where self-help ends. By 'self-help' I mean efforts by the participants to solve the problems themselves, without enlisting external help.

Figure 6.5 shows how far the different forms of help can go.

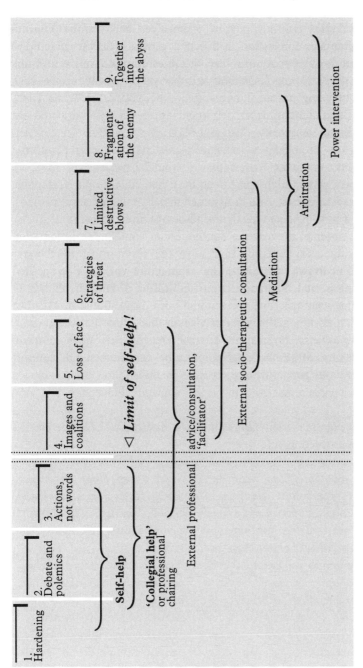

Figure 6.5: The nine levels of escalation and different forms of help

Even if the conflict parties themselves are trained conflict consultants or counsellors, self-help is generally only feasible up to the threshold of escalation level 4. On escalation levels 4 or 5 any attempt at self-help is difficult because the opponents accuse each other of being partial. I have often experienced this when I was involved in conflict myself. My opponent could not and would not grant me the authority to suggest methods for tackling the conflict. Doing so – so he felt – would have placed me in a superior position! And my opponent feared that I would have chosen my own methods, which might have been most beneficial to me personally, as I knew them best. And he assumed that, by using my own methods, I would have exploited my 'home advantage' in this match.

In order to prevent the conflict about conflict resolution from hindering every attempt to resolve the situation, a third party should be drawn in straightaway – somebody who can't be accused of being partial. The conflict parties still have the difficult task of agreeing what exactly a professional third party should be asked to do. Chapter 8 contains some advice on this.

Let us remind ourselves here that 'collegial help' does not mean counselling by professional advisers or consultants, but support from neutral people who are trusted by the conflict parties. How a conflict party might go about this is shown in Figure 6.6.

In the examples 'Boilerworks plc' and 'Erasmus School' the parties might proceed as follows:

The mechanics and their boss agree to ask for help from a representative of the works council and a departmental manager from a different plant. These two people are to conduct talks with them and to lead a joint discussion. Both colleagues are prepared to provide this help.

Neither the works council representative nor the other

Several key people from the young 'Progressives' and the 'ProArt' group independently contact several colleagues from two other alternative schools, A and B. They once met these people in training sessions and now ask them for help. These people are prepared to help, as long as no one raises objections against the particular people

departmental manager are experts in conflict management. But they once attended a course on communication skills and are considered by the conflict parties to have integrity and impartiality. They have no personal interest in the conflict, even though they work in the same company and are thus part of the overall system.

named. This is reported during one of the weekly staff meetings in the Erasmus School, and a list of names is presented. Each party chooses the head teacher, Derek, from School A and a teacher, Lena, from School B. Both these people have the confidence of both parties.

Figure 6.6: Enlisting collegial help

These days many people attend courses on communication skills, and many staff and managers have been trained in handling conflict. Even if this isn't their job, e.g. in an internal personnel or other organizational capacity, they can serve their colleagues or friends well. If they recognize that their help isn't sufficient either, they can at least advise on what exactly a professional consultant should be asked to do.

The importance of collegial help in conflict resolution is likely to increase in the near future. In the healthcare environment there are already many self-help groups of people who are in similar situations and who want and are able to help one another. However, it is always vital to keep in mind the limits of self-help and collegial help.

7. What can I do myself at the different escalation levels?

This chapter introduces the most important methods that can be used by people involved in conflict, even if they don't have any professional training. Up to level 3 this work can be undertaken independently, as self-help, like self-medication, whereas from level 4 onwards, collegial help is required to tackle conflicts. From level 5 onwards professional advisers and mediators must be brought in. My book on conflict management[1] was written for these people, which is why instructions for external 'third parties' are only touched on in the material which follows.

7.1 At escalation level 1: hardening

Once again, the most important characteristics of the first level of escalation can be summarized as follows:

- Positions increasingly harden and clash.
- Occasional glitches lead to bias on both sides.
- Awareness of the tensions that exist causes spasm.[2]
- People still believe that the tension can be resolved through talking!
- Parties and factions are not yet entrenched.
- People are still more prepared to co-operate than to be competitive.

Figure 7.1: Main characteristics of escalation level 1

The main aims of the key techniques on this level are as follows:
1. People stop arguing about the reasons for and background to the conflict, *concentrating instead on the disputed core issues.*
2. Good *methods of communication* relieve strain in the dispute.

3. *Loosening and dissolving the spasm* helps the conflict partners to bring their positive qualities to bear once again.

(1) Concentrating on the key issues in the dispute

Of course all conflicts focus on contentious issues: first these are factual differences; later differences over personal characteristics and interpersonal relationships also come into play. Therefore it is important to clarify which points the parties disagree on. Each party sees these points slightly differently, considers their importance differently and insists that what is in dispute is only what they experience, nothing else.

Therefore one of the first steps is to list and compare the contentious issues (Figure 7.2) from the different viewpoints of each party. One of the people involved will begin this process and, if she does so sensitively, she can get the other side to open up. In this way a consensus can be reached about exactly what the contentious issues are. If nothing else, this should mean that there can no longer be any controversy about which questions should be tackled.

One side can introduce discussion about the contentious issues in the following way:

1. Show your interest in clarifying the contentious issues. Suggest that initially all you want to do is to establish, calmly, what the contentious issues are. Working on the conflict itself will come later. Naming the contentious issues doesn't mean making any decisions, it is merely intended to guide the encounter back on track. Emphasize that in the following points you are merely presenting your subjective view of things.

2. Explain: 'For me (or for us as a group) these are the contentious issues which we should look at and work on: ...' Don't give the contrasting stances, simply name the 'headings' of the contentious issues and invite the opposing side to ask clarifying questions.
   Ensure that no statements are made for or against the different positions! Restrict yourself to simply listing the headings – as in the table of contents of a book.

3. Invite the opposing side to give the headings for the contentious issues from their point of view. Ask clarifying questions if you haven't understood a point made. But don't be tempted into discussing content as yet. First you need to agree on the priorities.
4. Confirm to the opposing party that you have taken note of the contentious issues that have been named. And ask your counterpart to confirm in turn that she has heard and understood the points you raised. Write down the issues.
5. Jointly go through the two lists. Discuss which points are similar and where the parties are likely to be concerned about different issues. For the time being the important thing is to acknowledge common points and differences.

Figure 7.2: Gathering and examining contentious issues[3]

This method can at least ensure that the parties are not solely fixated on their own view of the issues. As soon as they open up towards one another, issues of content can be discussed.

There are several variations for gathering and examining contentious issues, as for example the following:

- Blank cards are used to collect the points. First each side writes down their own points on a card, and these are then pinned up on a board and compared. With this method there is least chance of the participants influencing each other.
- Or: Invite the opposing side to talk, initially giving only three issues; then you give three issues. Then it's the other side's turn to raise another three points, then yours, etc., until the list is more or less complete. With this method you can prevent one party raising their points simply in reaction to what was brought up by the other side.

There is then a very simple method to reach agreement about the priority given to the issues:

- Give the opposing side the opportunity to select two issues from **your** list for discussion.
- Then it's your turn to choose two points from the **opposing side's list.**

In this way it is not possible for one party to impose their issues on the other side; instead, the issues of both sides are recognized and tackled.

(2) Suitable methods of communication relieve the strain in the dispute

Once you have agreed on the issues, it is advisable to begin by discussing the less emotive questions in order to achieve a few successes. This will then encourage people to tackle the more difficult issues as well.

When discussing the contentious issues, the aim is to dissolve temporary hardening and spasm. The following method (Figure 7.3) softens rigid positions. If the differences are about big, global issues, these should be broken down into several 'dimensions'.

Using the example of 'Boilerworks plc':
The leader of the maintenance team is dissatisfied with the way in which decisions are reached in the team meetings. He offers his staff the opportunity to discuss the issue of 'decision-making' and proceeds as follows:

1. Once they have identified the issue of 'team decision-making' as the prime contentious issue, they break down the big, global issue into different aspects: basic decisions – technical decisions – personnel decisions – work planning – budget decisions.
2. They agree to tackle the issue of 'work planning' as the first aspect.
3. Before they begin to discuss the chosen aspect, they jointly break it down into further components, its logical 'dimensions':
   a) How are staff informed about jobs that come up?
   b) How are the targets for the coming week communicated?
   c) How are tasks broken down?
   d) How are the tasks allocated to suitable people?
   e) How do the mechanics themselves organize the way in which they work together?

f) What help do the mechanics receive in problem situations?

g) How are results (quality, time, costs) monitored?

h) How does the team leader receive feedback?

4. The group decides to look at sub-points b and d.

5. On sub-point b (information about weekly targets) the mechanics describe how they see things going at present, where they perceive problems and what they want to change and how. Their boss asks clarifying questions but does not comment.

6. The team leader presents his view of things and the problems he perceives with sub-point b (information about weekly targets) and explains what he might be able to contribute to resolve the issue.

7. The group examines the negative and positive consequences of both approaches to resolve the situation and agrees on the preferred solution. The result is written down, along with a brief explanation of the criteria.

Figure 7.3: Dissolving spasm by 'dimensionalizing contentious issues' [4]

By breaking down the issue into components and 'dimensionalizing' it, the real core questions become more apparent and are defined more accurately. As the people involved listen calmly to the explanations and suggestions, the avalanche of generalized contentious issues melts away until only manageable, specific points remain. The same approach is taken with the other sub-points.

In addition, the methods described in Chapter 6 (articulating feelings, hopes and fears) can also be useful on escalation level 1. This approach brings the reality of feelings, assumptions, insinuations etc. from semi-darkness into the light of people's awareness.

There are often tensions in the analysis of problems, or in decision-making, because the various steps are taken in the wrong order.

Figure 7.4 shows the order in which the basic elements should be discussed.

If a group is to analyse a problem (recognition) or if a decision for an action is to be made (will), it will follow similar steps along the way:

Two types of problem-solving approaches:

Analysis of the problem **Recognition**	**Decision, resolution** **Will, action**

Step 1 is the same for both:

1. Preparation (planning and group formation)

What is our problem? It is best to phrase this as a question: 'What leads to ...? What is the cause of ...?'
What is the aim of this discussion?
Are there any pre-determined conditions or frameworks?
What preparation is necessary?
How do we structure the time? Who leads the discussion?
Who takes on other functions?
Which procedure do we want to adopt?

2. Image-building

Gathering facts, observations, opinions, suppositions, viewpoints; the view broadens; don't discuss, judge or evaluate anything – just collect the information!	Gathering possible approaches; clarifying ideas and suggestions; clarifying pre-given ideas and criteria; don't discuss anything, just collect the alternatives!

---

3. Process of judgement

Comparison: Where are there similarities and differences? What's in the foreground, what in the background? Hypotheses, i.e. suggest and discuss possible explanations	Discuss criteria and determine their priorities; discuss alternatives and compare them against criteria; check the consequences of the alternatives

4. Conclusion

Critically test hypotheses, narrow down; selection of the most plausible explanation; securing results (reasons); sorting out the documentation, checking agreement	Critically check preferred solutions against criteria; securing results (documentation); sorting out implementation, checking conclusion is binding!

Figure 7.4: Steps in problem-solving or decision-making discussions[5]

Often there is a hardening and spasm in discussions for, in their own thoughts, the people involved are at different stages of the discussion; or because they want to work on the steps at different speeds and with different degrees of detail; or maybe they want to achieve conclusions too quickly. If the steps of image-building and forming a judgement have not progressed far enough (when people jump to conclusions), others will feel steam-rollered, taken by surprise or cornered if somebody is urging for a conclusion.

Each step in this process requires different qualities, which are connected with the archaic, early Christian elements of *fire, light/ air, water* and *earth:*

Step 1 'Preparation': The problem to be solved becomes the real concern of those involved; *warmth* is created for the problem and for one another. A 'cold start' would inevitably lead to a result with which nobody can identify. The main requirements are clarity about the way forward and commitment to the approach to solving the problem.

Step 2 'Image-building': *Light* is shed on the matter; it is x-rayed; perspectives emerge. Here the discussion should be broad so that it doesn't get stuck with first ideas, which may be on the wrong track.

Step 3 'Process of judgement': The quality of *water* is at work here, creating flow, connecting, dissolving and re-connecting. In this phase there must be real controversy, openness and directness in discussion.

Step 4 'Conclusion': People must gain firm ground under their feet; points that had previously been open must be given shape now. The alternatives are definitively narrowed down; focus is needed rather than breadth. The most important thing is that the people involved are able to stand by the solution that is found.

(3) Loosening allows a return to the positive qualities of the people involved

On the first level of escalation a lot can still be done to loosen the dispute. You should take care not to 'personify' the controversies triggered by the organization, i.e. not allow certain people to be given sole blame for the disagreements. This was covered in Chapters 1 and 3.

7.2 At escalation level 2: debate and polemics

After the threshold to the second level of escalation (see Figure 5.3), the following main characteristics emerge:

- The differences are aired in arguments and polemics.
- The dispute is governed by polarization in thinking, feelings and will.
- 'Either/or' thinking controls everything.
- Cunning verbal tactics are used: people pretend to argue rationally – but are using verbal violence.
- People try to gain recognition by 'speaking to an audience', i.e. by involving third parties.

- Groupings and factions form around different stances; these groupings vary in their composition and do not last.
- Discrepancies between 'overtone' and 'undertone' lead to confusion and scepticism.
- There is fighting for dominance (TA model).
- The attitudes of co-operation and competitiveness oscillate continuously and increase confusion.

Figure 7.5: Main characteristics of escalation level 2

The methods which follow are aimed to achieve the following:
1. *To uncover the polarizing powers* that operate on level 2, to see through them and to disable them.
2. To turn the fight for dominance into a *debate between partners.*
3. To enable the conflict parties *to get away from the compulsive game of ping-pong* and once again be self-directed.

Apart from the methods described here, the approaches already described for escalation level 1 are also still effective.

(1) Disabling the polarizing powers
Through the method of 'alter ego' comment,[6] disrupting discrepancies between 'overtones' and 'undertones' can be made audible (Figure 7.6). This helps to disperse the confusion arising from a constant interchange of ambiguities.

The aim of this method is two-fold: it is intended to enable you to empathize with the feelings and attitudes of other people, and to give space for emotions in interpersonal encounters. Using the example of the 'Erasmus School', it might look like this:

1. At the beginning of a meeting the head teacher agrees on a rule with the teachers: by raising a hand, each member of the group can interrupt the discussion at any time in order to articulate what she thinks the emotions or mood of a colleague are; after the meeting there is feedback on how the technique was experienced.

2. After a few minutes Anthony says: 'Alter ego for Bridget: "I am annoyed that no one has responded to my concerns!" – is that right, Bridget?'
3. Bridget confirms: 'It's 90 per cent true.'
4. After several contributions Christine gives a hand signal: 'Alter ego for David: "I'm cross because Bridget is putting words into my mouth. I didn't mean that" – is that right David?'
5. David: 'Exactly!'

Figure 7.6: 'Alter ego' comment

'Alter ego' comments dissolve the spasm that developed, and at the same time they have preventive effects. They make it possible to experience the aspect of social interaction that is otherwise hidden, often suppressed, and which – because of this – becomes a source of problems.

It is particularly important – but also difficult! – to make people aware of unfair debating tactics and of the use of verbal violence. To do this, you first need to know what these tactics are[7] and to recognize them. But often people have a vague feeling that there might be something wrong with the logic of an argument, without being able to say exactly what the problem is. To point out such tactics, it is enough to give a clear signal in the form of an I-message:

'I get a bad feeling here!'

'Something doesn't feel right to me!'

'I don't know why, but that doesn't sound completely logical to me!'

'I don't quite understand – I can't follow that thought!'

Incidentally, it has been shown that the people who are most successful in court trials are those who are least afraid to admit that they don't understand something. Saying you don't understand something is linked to a request to explain and clarify once more, and this prevents hasty and polarizing responses. The exchange is no longer so hectic but becomes calmer.

Your own feelings are an important yardstick for measuring appropriate behaviour: do you feel increasingly driven into a corner? Are you still able to relax whenever you want? Can you still breathe calmly when you get into difficulty? Are you feeling increasingly other-directed? It can be very helpful to ask for a break in the discussion, or to postpone the decision to the next day to give people a chance to 'sleep on it'. This creates space – physical and thinking space.

If either/or thinking has already driven the viewpoints far apart into extreme positions, a game-like method can awaken awareness for the shades between black and white. However, unless it is used carefully, the 'rubber band' method described in Figure 7.7[8] can be somewhat risky because playful and deliberate polarization can become serious. The person guiding or facilitating the exercise must therefore try out the technique for herself before doing it in the group.

It should be pointed out that deliberately increasing polarization is intended to tease out the intermediate positions that are often overlooked. If you are unsure, it is best to enlist collegial help. Several extreme viewpoints are selected from the contentious issues. In the conflict experienced by 'Boilerworks plc' these might be the different views about the new and the old maintenance system: the mechanics defend the existing system under which repairs are carried out according to a scheme devised by the maintenance department itself, as this leads to less downtime overall; the team leader on the other hand defends a new system of preventive maintenance that is aligned with production schedules.

I call this technique the 'rubber band' method because deliberately exaggerating the polarized stances, and the explanations provoked by it, increases the 'pull towards the centre'. The opponents resist the more extreme stances and, through their explanations ('I don't want that either! That would be going much too far!'), refute some of the things they have been accused of, at least implicitly. All too often one side secretly harbours the suspicion that the other party might take even more extreme stances if it weren't meeting with resistance.

1. The mechanics and the team leader agree to play the game, and that they will not as yet make any decisions; they only want to find out the arguments for and against the two systems. The team leader and one of the mechanics jointly lead the discussion.

M   L

Current position of the
mechanics: maintenance plans
80% of repairs; ad hoc repairs
are always deferred

Current position of the team
leader: under his system 80%
of work is aligned with
production schedules

2. The team leader encourages the mechanics to imagine a more extreme stance he might take; the mechanics oblige.

L → **L1**

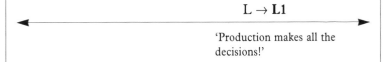

'Production makes all the
decisions!'

3. The team leader invites the mechanics, to imagine an even more extreme stance he might take; the mechanics oblige.

L → L1 → **L2**

'Production treats
maintenance like slaves!'

4. The team leader explains what he objects to in positions L1 and L2: 'I don't want to hand over responsibility to production; I want production and maintenance to agree on joint aims and priorities'

5. The team leader describes what more extreme positions taken by the mechanics might sound like:

M1 ← M

'The mechanics want to tell
production what to produce
and when ...'

6. The mechanics now give their thoughts on M1 (and M2): 'We never want to be the super bosses of the production managers! We don't want to control production autocratically. But we don't want to be ordered around all the time.'

7. The explanations of the team leader and the mechanics thus show up intermediate positions between the original viewpoints.

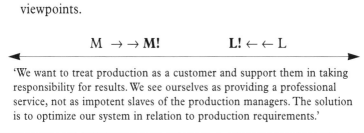

M → → **M!**   **L!** ← ← L

'We want to treat production as a customer and support them in taking responsibility for results. We see ourselves as providing a professional service, not as impotent slaves of the production managers. The solution is to optimize our system in relation to production requirements.'

Figure 7.7: Increasing the opposing stances: 'rubber band' method

(2) From fighting for dominance to a debate between partners
Often people are kept from acting prudently by their fear that the other side might think them weak. And this might endanger the high regard other people have for them. The emerging concern with prestige therefore acts as a stimulus for escalation. On escalation level 2 the opponents begin the game for real: 'Who is superior? Who is inferior?' Keep asking yourself whether you have to prove your superiority to yourself and your counterpart by trying to push her into an inferior position. Do you need to devalue the other party in order to increase your own sense of value? If the actions of the other side give you the impression that you are not treated as an equal partner but are lectured to like a silly 'child', then you can say so:
    'I don't feel taken seriously as a partner!'
    'I feel as if I had to look up to you – this restricts me.'
    'I notice how I am beginning to think in terms of superior and inferior – I don't want that.'

(3) From compulsive ping-pong to self-directed action
The polarization can generally be defused by
- slowing down rather than speeding up the debate,
- offering and seeking space for reflection,
- adding colour between the extremes of black and white, and
- seeking and offering equality rather than dominance.

All these methods help the Everyday Ego regain the ability to listen to its own Light personality – which speaks more quietly than the Shadow personality (see Chapter 2) – and the discussion loses its compulsive character. Over-hasty reactions are once again replaced by prudent, self-directed action, and the frantically inflamed beat gives way to a lively rhythm.

7.3 At escalation level 3: actions, not words

As the differences couldn't be settled through polemical debate, the following key features are apparent at the third level:

- Talking no longer helps: actions must therefore show what it's all about!
- The opponents confront each other with *faits accomplis.*
- There are discrepancies between verbal statements and non-verbal behaviour; non-verbal behaviour has a greater effect than the spoken word.
- Insecurity is created through the risk of misinterpreting actions.
- Pessimistic expectations rooted in suspicion accelerate the conflict.
- The parties move closer together, build barriers around themselves and exclude people who don't share their thinking.
- A 'group skin' forms and increases the pressure for conformity.
- Crystallizing of roles leads to specialization, entrenchment and restrictions.
- The conflict parties largely lose empathy.
- Competitiveness is stronger than co-operation.

Figure 7.8: Main characteristics of escalation level 3

There are three important keys to conflict resolution at this level:

1. *Strengthening empathy:* This re-opens doors to the other party, so that fantasies about the opposing party's evil intentions are no longer fed.
2. *Loosening the crystallized roles* so that these do not turn into clichéd enemy images.
3. Clarifying the perceived *discrepancies between verbal and non-verbal messages.*

(1) Strengthening empathy

Several of the methods introduced so far serve to recognize and articulate the emotional dimension: constructive confrontation (Figures 1.6 to 8), I-messages (Figure 6.3) and 'alter ego' comments (Figure 7.6), as well as articulating non-values (Figure 6.4). The approaches which follow (Figure 7.9 and 7.10) are best used in a group. They strengthen empathy with the thoughts, feelings and will of the opposing party.

As a group, select an occasion where you were unable to understand and approve of the behaviour of the opposing side:

1. Begin by jointly recalling the events (details are very useful too), but without making any judgements.
2. List the individuals from the opposing side who acted as 'key figures': 'Anthony, Bridget and Chrissie.'
3. For about 10 minutes several members of the group (the 'Anthonys') identify only with Anthony whilst others merely listen and note down the statements. All the 'Anthonys' articulate in the first person the things Anthony might have thought, felt and wanted in this situation. Whenever somebody says something negative, the next person must make a positive statement; then another negative statement can be made, etc. It is okay if the statements are contradictory.
4. For the next 10 minutes another part of the group (the 'Bridgets') identifies only with Bridget whilst the others make notes. All the 'Bridgets' say in the first person what Bridget might have thought, felt and wanted. Once again, a negative statement is followed by a positive statement by the next person. Contradictions are allowed.

5. Yet another set of people identifies with Chrissie for 10 minutes; the others note down the I-messages about this person. Negative and positive statements alternate.
6. Share your thoughts: which statements were new for you, which had you not expected in this way? How easy or difficult did you find it to come up with positive statements as well? What did you feel?
7. What would you need to change in your own behaviour in order to do something about the things you were able to experience in this exercise?

Figure 7.9: Identifying with the opposing party[9]

It is important not to allow yourself to be tempted into uttering only negative fantasies about the opposing side. After the exercise you can see your own group through the eyes of the opposing group. Talk about how you think your opponent would talk about you. Once you have empathized with the opposing party in this way, ask yourself: what obstacles prevent an exchange with the other party? Where might the difficulties lie? What could you do to overcome them?

The following method of role reversal (Figure 7.10)[10] helps to prepare an encounter with the other party.

In the 'Erasmus School' conflict the role reversal is practised as follows:

Anne from the 'ProArt' group takes on the role of Bridget (key figure in the 'Progressives' group) and David (key figure in the 'Progressives' group) plays the role of Christopher, a member of the 'ProArt' group.

1. For about seven minutes Anne plays the role of Bridget (Progressives) and takes her position that more IT teaching is required; David plays Christopher's role (ProArt), advocating the view of his own party.

They discuss the contentious issues: how the teachers should be addressed by the pupils; how the children behave in the breaks; eating and drinking during lessons etc.

The other group members observe the exercise, with one person responsible for keeping an eye on the time and ensuring the rules are followed.

2. The time-keeper interrupts and asks Anne (ProArt) and David (Progressives) to slip back into their own roles. They continue the dispute where it had been interrupted for the role reversal, acting as if they had always played exactly the same role they are playing now.

3. After another seven minutes or so the time-keeper ends the game. The participants reflect on their experiences, describing how they found the role reversal. Anne, David and the observers summarize what now appears understandable, acceptable and justified in the stance taken by each opposing party.

Figure 7.10: Role reversal

The effect of this exercise increases with the number of people who get to experience the role change. Role change could also be attempted with the different parties actually sitting opposite each other. But don't expect miracles: in real conflicts the effect of the role change rarely goes very deep. However, as an exercise for increasing empathy, it is a very valuable technique.

(2) Loosening the crystallized roles

The increasing crystallization of roles restricts certain people to only a few key contributions and, over time, leads to clichéd images of the enemy. In this situation the simple role-negotiation method (Figure 7.11) can help.

In one variant the two partners don't write down their wishes in advance but list them there and then in a conversation and negotiate afterwards. They should deliberately conduct the negotiation on a factual basis and give each other equal chances.

Using the example of 'Boilerworks plc', roles between the team leader and the senior mechanic might be negotiated in the following way:

1. The team leader (working on his own) formulates three basic wishes (a–c):
   In order for me to do my job better, I want the following from the senior mechanic:
   a) He should *do the following more often,* or *he should start doing the following new things:*
   – immediately pass on to me any breakdown reports
   – pull me in as soon as possible when there are differences with the production managers
   – intervene directly with the supplies manager when the supplies department provides insufficient support
   b) He should do the following *less frequently* or *not at all:*
   – try to agree a decision with the mechanics before team meetings
   – spread cynical comments about absurd rules
   – use delaying tactics
   c) He should *continue to do* the following:
   – check the quality of his colleagues' work
   – be responsible for allocating shifts in the team
   – make light-hearted remarks when team meetings become tense.
   At the same time the senior mechanic also writes down his own wishes, a, b and c, in relation to the team leader.

2. The senior mechanic and the team leader exchange papers and read each other's wishes.

3. The senior mechanic and the team leader ask clarifying questions, but they do not discuss whether or not they consider the wishes justified.

4. The senior mechanic explains which wishes he wants to grant, provided the team leader also grants *his* most important

wishes. The team leader selects the wishes of the mechanic he is prepared to grant. The two agree to fulfil four wishes from the mechanic's list and from the team leader's list.

5. This agreement is written down and both sign their name next to the wishes. Each partner receives a copy of the two sheets, and the two agree a date for a progress review.

Figure 7.11: Role-negotiation in pairs[11]

Figure 7.12 offers another variant. It quickly delivers very useable results in a group situation. The conflict parties can work together in the same room. If the group consists of no more than about 14 people, the whole process can be completed in about two to three hours.

1. Each person pins up a flip chart sheet and writes her *own name* at the top. Apart from the name, only the following items are written on the sheet:
    a) *Please start doing the following things/do the following things more often:*   (space for writing)

    b) *Please don't do the following any more, or do it to a lesser extent:*   (space for writing)

    c) *Please don't change the following:*
                            (space for writing)

2. Each person then goes from one sheet to the next and writes in the spaces on the sheet what behaviour she wants from the others. The name of the 'wisher' is clearly written after each wish. If others have the same wishes, they simply add their name. Everyone can go to the same sheet more than once, adding new wishes.
    This stage is conducted in silence, lasting around 20 minutes. A signal is given at the end.

3. Now Anthony goes to his flip chart, reads out all the wishes and asks clarifying questions. There is no discussion of the wishes. Anthony then signs his name against the wishes he wants to and is able to grant. He only agrees to items he is confident of being able to achieve.

4. Then Bridget goes to her flip chart, reads out the wishes, asks clarifying questions, agrees her promises and confirms by signing her name.

5. At the end the participants agree a date for a progress review to which each will bring their flip chart.

6. At the progress review the participants check which promises can be considered as 'kept' and where new promises are necessary or desirable.

Figure 7.12: Role-negotiation in group situations[12]

The following points are important for the quality of the agreements made:
- Only specific behaviour should be described ('Greet the people in the workshop in the mornings!'), not wishes about people's general attitudes ('Be friendly').
- When the wishes are explained, people should not talk about occasions when problematic behaviour was observed; there is no discussion of the past, only of the future.
- There is no discussion about whether or not a wish is justified or meaningful; the only interesting thing is which wishes are to be granted.
- In order to maintain a balance, one side should not make many more concessions than the other.
- Each side can ask for a break if it thinks there is a danger of imbalance.

This method has a deliberately tight structure. Therefore it is generally possible for a member of the conflict parties to chair the discussion without any great risks. In a two-party conflict it is certainly better to agree on two people ('double chair') from the different sides to chair the encounter, and if three parties are involved, a 'triple chair' would be a good idea. In this way the discussion cannot be suspected of being misused by any one party to further its own interests.

(3) Clarifying discrepancies between verbal and non-verbal messages

As soon as there are fewer face-to-face conversations between the conflict parties because they meet each other with too much scepticism, the perception of the opponent becomes restricted. The discrepancies between words and actions lead each side to suspect hidden negative intentions on the part of the opposite party. Therefore you should try to ensure that your own behaviour clearly shows what your intentions are and what you *don't* want. For this purpose the 'non-values' (Figure 6.4) could be clearly articulated. It is advisable to raise possible misinterpretations yourself ('prolepsis', see Chapter 6) and to do everything you can to prevent lack of clarity about your actions from leading to 'pessimistic anticipation' (Chapter 4, Section C.1).

Face-to-face discussion between the parties is the best method to achieve this. With larger groups the key figures of the different camps can meet to seek clarification, but they must continually remind themselves that their perceptions are biased, distorted and skewed. This means that they must not take their subjective perception to be the objective truth. It is important to remember this in a face-to-face encounter, otherwise there is a danger that the discussion intensifies the conflict even further. The 'lead-in sentences' offered in Figure 7.13 emphasize the possibility of such distorted perceptions.

These lead-in sentences are also important if both conflict parties give different descriptions of the situation. Both are convinced that their version is the whole truth, and both also believe that the other side is lying by describing events differently. In fact both could win by finding out what the world looked like when seen through different eyes.

The events of the conflict are always perceived and interpreted subjectively and from one viewpoint only – that is, in a biased way. If a conversation about critical events takes place between the parties, they should always be aware of the fact that their own subjectivity is the most natural thing in the world.

When describing events, try to start with the following types of phrases as often as possible:
- 'I saw this in the following way ...'
- 'In my perception the following happened ...'
- 'As far as I remember, the whole thing went this way ...'
- 'I had the impression that ...'
- 'To me it looked as if ...'

Intervene to correct the other side if they fall back on statements such as 'This is what happened, don't tell me otherwise ...' or 'What really happened is ...'. Point out that each person's view is determined by where she sits and the position she takes.

Figure 7.13: Lead-in sentences for statements of perception

An effective method to make people aware that their view of things is determined by the stance they take is described, for example, in Steiner's lectures *Human and Cosmic Thought*.[13] This method can help to overcome the distortion of our perception and the corruption of our faculty of perception which occur in conflict situations. Imagine a triangle inside a circle, i.e. within a circle that always encloses all three corners of the triangle; next imagine one corner moving along the arc of the circle. Then you can imagine another corner of the triangle moving along the arc. This continually changes the shape of the triangle: it shifts and is seen from a different perspective all the time. You can carry out a similar exercise with a globe. It looks different viewed from the North Pole than from the South Pole. Each perspective is justified in some way, neither is actually wrong. In Australia there are maps of the world on which the South Pole is shown at the top and the North Pole at the bottom. Europeans will have difficulty recognizing many countries when they are viewed 'upside down'.

Their stance determines people's outlook and thus also their view of the world. In the same way the same basic thought takes a different form in each soul. However, I must practise seeing through the eyes of my fellow human beings as well, and they in turn can be invited to try seeing things from my angle. Training flexibility in perception and thinking opens up different viewpoints which had previously been overlooked or excluded.

There are certainly many other useful methods as well. But the techniques described here are of key importance as they tackle the patterns and mechanisms of attitudes and behaviour which characterize this level.

This is where we reach the limits of self-help. Good-quality collegial help does, of course, make sense at this stage as well and can be very helpful. With collegial help, some of the methods for the fourth escalation level can therefore be used on level 3 as well.

7.4 At escalation level 4: images and coalitions

As a reminder, here are the main features of escalation level 4 once more; concern about each party's own image and efforts to gain support are the central features.

- The disagreement is dominated by stereotypical images, by clichés in relation to knowledge and abilities, by image campaigns and rumours.
- The parties manoeuvre each other into negative roles and fight these roles.
- They woo for support, as weakness leads to a need for support.
- Self-fulfilling prophesies through fixation on biased and distorted enemy images confirm these images.
- Provocation, snide remarks and annoyance are done so cleverly that they are hard to prove.
- 'Double bind' through paradoxical orders creates interlocking.

Figure 7.14: Main characteristics of escalation level 4

As soon as the conflict parties have created strongly distorted images of each other, they can no longer help themselves. They are constantly open to the suspicion that they are merely pursuing their own interests. They are enemies and no longer believe that the other party is honestly prepared to improve relations. In such situations it is very useful if the parties can at least agree to enlist collegial help or the advice of external conflict advisors.

As collegial help is offered by non-professional people, I will now describe several key methods for this level of conflict. These also represent important interventions for professional advisers or consultants working at level 4.

The following example methods have three aims:
1. They make biased and *distorted perceptions* conscious and allow for an exchange and *correction* of these perceptions.
2. The *perceptive mechanisms* which led to filtering and distortion are to be recognized and *disabled*.
3. The conflict parties *free themselves from fateful role attributions* into which they have manoeuvred each other.

(1) Correcting distorted perceptions which disable perceptive mechanisms

Each side suffers because the opposing party has created a distorted image of it, stunting its identity. However, neither side notices that it has done exactly the same to the enemy. These distorted images exert powerful control over events. The method described in Figure 7.15 has the effect of making visible to the other side the enemy images and self-images that were previously hidden. It is only by making these images visible that they can be corrected and removed.

The teaching staff of the 'Erasmus School' had enlisted collegial help from the head teacher, Derek, and a teacher, Lena, from two other alternative schools, A and B. Lena and Derek agreed to provide help and invited the two parties to work on bringing out each party's self-image and image of the other party, and to present these images to each other. They proceeded as follows:

'Progressives' party:	**'ProArt' party:**
Meeting separately, the group writes down:	Meeting separately, the group writes down:

1. How they see the ProArt group:
   – creative – but conservative
   – dogmatic in their arguments
   – removed from reality
   – ...
	1. How they see the 'Progressives' group:
	   – intelligent – but superficial
	   – intent on pleasing the parents
	   – lacking pedagogical depth
	   – ...

2. How they see themselves:
   – challenging
   – open
   – pragmatic
   – ...
	2. How they see themselves:
	   – personality-oriented
	   – responsible
	   – open
	   – ...

3. Joint meeting – exchange of images of the other party:
The *Progressives* group presents how it sees the ProArt group. The ProArt group asks questions: 'What do you mean by 'removed from reality'? Please give us some specific examples.'

4. The *ProArt* group presents how it sees the Progressives group;
the Progressives group asks clarifying questions and requests specific examples.

Meeting separately,	Meeting separately,
5. The *Progressives* group compares the image of the Progressives presented by ProArt with its own self-image: Why does the ProArt group see us in this way? What have we ourselves contributed to this image? What do we need to change so that this image is no longer created?	5. The *ProArt* group compares the image of the ProArt group as presented by the Progressives with its own self-image: Why does the Progressives group see us in this way? What have we ourselves contributed to this image? What do we need to change so that this image is no longer created?

6. Joint meeting – exchange of the explanations and resolutions for the future:
   The *ProArt* group presents its explanations, asks for confirmation and suggestions, asks whether the changes in behaviour it has identified might have the desired effect.

7. The *Progressives* group presents its findings, asks for confirmation and suggestions and asks whether the changes in behaviour might have the desired effect.

8. Minutes and a progress review date are agreed jointly. Review of the meeting.

Figure 7.15: Clarifying self-image and image of the other [14]

Derek will lead the Progressives group in the separate discussions, Lena the ProArt party. By asking specific questions, they continuously point out the relativity of the subjective perceptions. Leading jointly, Derek and Lena ensure that, when the images of the other are presented, there is no protest, scornful laughter or derogatory remarks. Therefore they repeatedly emphasize that it is better to bring the images to the surface than to allow them to wreak havoc as ghosts and phantoms in semi-darkness. After all, it is these artificial images that get in people's way and fight each other – not the objective truths.

Three things will happen when confronting self-images with the images of the other:

1. It will become apparent that, for example, certain actions of the Progressives were perceived incorrectly by ProArt and interpreted negatively; the misperception can then be corrected.
2. It will transpire that, for example, actions by the Progressives created different effects than they had intended; they can then learn from feedback given by ProArt about these discrepancies, so that they can start to create a better fit between the intention and the effect of their deeds and words.
3. And it will become obvious that the Progressives had in fact intended certain effects, but that completely different *side effects* had also emerged, pushing the intended effects into the background.

In all three cases the people involved can only benefit from the feedback and exchange of images, as this can achieve a better fit between intentions and effects.

My technique of micro-analysis of a critical episode[15] described in Figure 7.16, has a similar aim. This approach builds on Figure 1.11 in Chapter 1. As critical events triggered incorrect conclusions and caused an increase in suspicion, a new basis for co-operation can be created by working on a number of episodes.

As Figure 7.16 shows, the approach moves from articulating the (1) effects of a certain behaviour to (2) the externally perceptible behaviour before uncovering (3) the inner, psychological aspects (the perception and thoughts, emotions and attitudes, intentions and aims). Thus, after articulating perceived effects, it progresses from the external factors on to the internal factors that contributed to the critical episode.

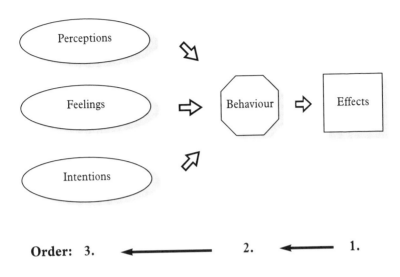

Figure 7.16: Conducting micro-analysis of a critical episode

The approach according to this method can be illustrated using the example of the 'Erasmus School'. Anne and Ben agree to work on an episode that occurred on 15 April in a meeting of subject heads. Ben had accused Anne – a very popular maths teacher – of pedagogical incompetence; Anne was very hurt and in response announced that she would leave the school. The rumour that she might hand in her notice had alarmed many parents.

Derek facilitates the discussion and begins as follows: 'Now let's look at what exactly happened on 15 April at 2.40 pm'. He starts with Anne (Figure 7.17).

This is the specific approach facilitated by Derek as a 'collegial moderator'.

1. Effects on Anne:

Derek: 'Anne, tell us what you felt about Ben's remarks!'

Anne describes her subjective impressions at the time: 'I felt very small ... At first I was completely confused and speechless ... Then I became very angry, my heart was beating as if it would burst ...'

Ben is asked to summarize Anne's remarks briefly, in his own words. No discussion or justification is allowed.

Anne confirms and, if necessary, adds to or corrects Ben's summary.

2. Ben's behaviour from Anne's perspective:

Derek: 'Anne, describe which aspects of Ben's behaviour were humiliating for you!'

Anne recalls: 'I remember his harsh tone of voice; I think Ben jumped up and shouted, towering over me; I had the impression that ...'

Ben briefly summarizes the aspects of his behaviour recalled by Anne and how she saw them. Again, there is no discussion or justification. Anne confirms or corrects Ben's summary.

3. Ben's behaviour from Ben's own perspective:

Derek: 'Ben, tell us which aspects of your behaviour you remember!'

Ben describes his behaviour: 'I jumped up and I think I first said that Anne's behaviour was driving me crazy; then I really did say in an icy tone of voice that I ...'

Derek asks Anne not to respond to this in any way but to summarize Ben's statement briefly. Anne does this.

Ben confirms that Anne's summary is correct.

4. Ben's inner motives as he remembers them:

Derek: 'Ben, tell us how you yourself experienced the situation at the time: which perceptions, feelings and intentions played an important role in this situation?'

Ben recalls: 'I had just had a difficult interview with parents; they had threatened to take their two children from the school. I was very stressed and couldn't take the pressure any longer. When Anne said ...'
Anne briefly summarizes Ben's statements.
Ben confirms.

5. **Steps 1 to 4** are repeated, but this time starting with Ben
   (1) describing the *effects* on him of Anne's behaviour,
   (2) describing Anne's *behaviour* as he remembers it,
   (3) then Anne adds what she remembers about her own *behaviour*,
   (4) and Anne continues by describing her *inner motives* in the situation (perceptions, emotions and feelings, intentions and aims).

6. **The cycle can start again at 1 with Anne.**

Figure 7.17: Micro-analysis of a critical episode

If this method is carried out carefully, precisely and with discipline, many points become clear. However, small details must be taken very seriously and minutely scrutinized. This is why I talk about a micro-analysis. In this way misunderstandings can be resolved; unwanted side-effects of emotional overreactions are recognized, as are the effects of earlier events which had been taken from one situation into the next 'undigested'. Many things have become mixed up which are actually unrelated. Thus the participants get to know the fateful discrepancies between their intentions and their behaviour, and between their behaviour and its actual effects.

At the end of the micro-analysis the participants can summarize their experiences (Figure 7.18).

I have repeatedly had the encouraging experience that even if a conflict has gone on for some time, has affected a large organization and produced many critical episodes, we still don't have to struggle through an endlessly drawn-out analysis of the whole story. If the critical episodes are selected carefully,[17] usually only three to five key episodes at the most have to be scrutinized precisely using the micro-analysis method. This is because the 'microcosm' of the critical episodes shows the essential elements of the 'macrocosm' of the conflict as a whole. Thoroughly working on these example episodes also means working on the conflict as a whole.

At the end of the micro-analysis Derek, the facilitator, asks Anne and Ben to comment on the following points:

1. Derek: 'Thinking back to the events of 15 April after these clarifications, what do you now regret most?'
   Ben: '... the fact that I rushed from that difficult discussion into the next meeting – without pausing to take breath – and then took out my anger on Anne.'
   Anne: '... the fact that I took Ben's anger personally and thought that he completely rejected me as a person. Now I realize that I provoked Ben even further by showing myself as helpless ...'

2. Derek: 'Drawing on what you have found out, what would you do differently if you were confronted with the same situation today?'
   Ben: 'I would say at the beginning of the meeting that I was feeling very stressed and needed the others to treat me considerately. And I would apologize immediately for my rude tone of voice.'
   Anne: 'I wouldn't swallow down my anger again but would openly admit that I was feeling hurt. I would ...'

3. Derek: 'What would you like to tell your colleague now? Say it to her/him directly.'
   Ben: 'I am sorry I was so inconsiderate ... I hope very much that you can forgive me, Anne ...'
   Anne: 'Ben, I want to tell you that I am ashamed that I turned it all into such a big deal afterwards. I hope that you can believe my explanation and that you will work with me again ...'

Figure 7.18: Learning from the past[16]

(2) Dissolving fateful role attributions

Collegial help or professional external support can dissolve fateful role attributions into which the conflict parties have manoeuvred each other. In this way they release each other from situations they have been forced into and give back each other's freedom to act.

The problem can be illustrated using the example of 'Boiler-works plc':

The mechanics accused their boss of a leadership style that was abhorrent to the team. And the team leader accused the mechanics of deliberately boycotting the new system because they didn't accept his authority as a manager. Each side thought that its behaviour was merely a response to the other side's behaviour. Each thought that it could only change its behaviour once the opposing side improved its own. In this way the opponents locked each other in fateful role attributions, with an 'unwritten role contract' which each side – subconsciously – strictly adhered to and monitored.

One method to resolve this interlocking is the 'U-Procedure' described in Figure 7.19.[18] The discussion begins by questioning the current situation and proceeds from specific practical things down to the deep, unwritten formulae of the relationship. The conflict parties then discuss how they want to shape their relationship in the future, returning to the specifics of the surface level. This method is called the 'U-Procedure' because of this movement from the visible surface down to the depths of the secret rules of the game and back again to the surface. It definitely requires good collegial help or professional support.

In 'Boilerworks plc', the works council representative, and the departmental manager, guide the discussion between the team of mechanics and their team leader.

The U-Procedure uncovers the beneficial as well as the hindering aspects of a relationship.

Current situation	Desired situation
1. What does the team leader do for the mechanics? What do the mechanics do for the team leader? The people involved list the 'core contributions' they have provided for each other so far.	7. What should the mechanics do for the team leader in the future? What should the team leader do for the mechanics? The people involved agree on the 'core contributions' each is to provide in the future.
2. What influence does the team leader have on the mechanics in this? What influence do the mechanics have on the team leader in this? What means do they use to exert pressure?	6. What influence should the mechanics have on the team leader in the future, and what influence should the team leader exert on the mechanics in the future? How could the two sides assert themselves?
3. What mottos might describe the current relationship between the mechanics and their boss? Which unwritten formula do they follow?	5. Which mottos should describe the relationship between the mechanics and the team leader in the future? What should the new 'contract formula' be?

4. Which mottos should remain? Which do we want to change, completely or partially?

Figure 7.19: U-Procedure to dissolve unwritten role contracts[19]

A few more details on the above:

The answers to Question 1 uncover the relationship between the conflict parties. 'Core contributions' means not only the work outputs for the company but also everything else that provides benefits for the other party. The mechanics: 'Because of our good professional performance the team leader was able to further his career; he could extend his influence within the plant; we provide back-up for him ...'

The answers to Question 2 show up the means – positive and negative (sanctions, rewards and punishments) – used by the parties to assert their will with the other.

Uncovering these forms of influence largely disables them. While working on Question 2, the participants can also discuss how they might increase these means of exerting pressure and how their interdependence might be increased further. This shows how the conflict parties hold each other locked into roles. Sometimes this can go as far as mutual blackmail.

The answers to Question 4 require a great deal of honesty and courage. The purpose is to name the unspoken 'secret rules of the game' which govern the way things go. It is therefore best to use brainstorming for this stage, in order to collect mottos, slogans, appeals etc. This should be done spontaneously, without censoring. The mottos are captured well if they contain an appeal for action or thinking: 'Queen takes Jack!', 'Safety first, then customer benefit!', 'Control is better than trust!' etc.

At escalation level 4 the limits of self-help and collegial help are reached. I will only indicate briefly what professional conflict consultancy should aim to do on the remaining levels to give the people involved in conflict an indication of what an adviser or counsellor might usefully do.

8. Professional help can go further!

You can use exercises from Chapter 3 to prepare yourself mentally for subsequent levels of conflict. This chapter highlights the exercises that are particularly useful for the various levels of escalation.

8.1 Forming a sounding board or contact group

If you have carried out some of these exercises, you can use the methods given in Chapter 6 to bring about a joint decision on external help. To do this, you can form a 'sounding board or contact group' (Figure 8.1), which can guide encounters between the different conflict parties and their future advisers in an orderly direction. It would be a shame if these encounters themselves gave rise to misunderstandings or suspicion, simply because some fundamental points had been disregarded. Figure 8.1 shows what is important.

This is how the conflict parties can successfully shape their first encounters with advisers:

1. *Each party on its own nominates* two of its members for the contact group (sounding board). The people involved decide for themselves, who belongs to which party. There should be no joint decision on this, otherwise the 'conflict about the conflict' (Chapter 1) might hinder further progress. It doesn't matter if one group is larger than another.
2. The people nominated to this group should be those who have already attempted to build bridges and who are recognized as *'moderates'* in terms of conducting the conflict, even if they have taken extreme positions in relation to content.

3. This group has *no decision-making powers;* it merely facilitates communication between the external advisers and the various conflict parties. The delegates of each group freely choose the most suitable way to communicate with their own and the other parties. (Of course a group can give decision-making mandates to the delegates.)
4. The members of the contact group give the appointed external advisers *direct access* to members of their own party.
5. If the organization releases *official information to the public,* this is agreed by the sounding board or contact group with their own parties and then released.
6. The contact group *checks the feasibility of the proposals* made by the appointed advisers.
7. The contact group *prepares the procedure for agreeing* the brief to the external advisers.
8. For the duration of the counselling, the contact group continues as the *partner for the external advisers.*
9. The contact group is *'first port of call for complaints'* about the counselling ('ombudsman function').

Figure 8.1: The sounding board or contact group[1]

It can make good sense to change one or two group members occasionally. This, too, is only decided by the conflict party who had previously nominated that person. Any change in the original tasks or competences of the sounding board or contact group has to be carried out very carefully and must be minuted in writing. This helps to reduce contentious issues in relation to the contact group itself to a minimum.

8.2 Briefing external advisers

In addition, the points listed in Figure 8.2 need to be considered when briefing external advisers or mediators.

During encounters with potential external advisers, the following
points need to be agreed:

a) The external advisers define *their role as well as the role of the
    conflict parties;* they describe which activities the conflict
    parties need to carry out themselves; the external advisers also
    explain *which roles they will not take on!*
b) The external advisers agree *rules* for future proceedings.
c) The external advisers clearly explain how they will deal with
    the *confidentiality* of the information they receive and how they
    will report on the progress of the counselling.
d) The external advisers outline their *ethical principles* for dealing
    with the conflict parties and give a binding commitment to
    keep to these principles.
e) The external advisers confirm in writing how they will deal
    with any *complaints* that may arise in relation to their work or
    in relation to any breaches of the established principles and
    rules; formal sanctions may be agreed against the external
    advisers in the event of any such breaches.
f) The external advisers outline a *step-by-step approach;* they
    describe which *'milestones'* are to be reached and when,
    insofar as this is possible after initial discussions.
g) The external advisers agree how they will conduct an
    assessment of interim results at the milestone points, and how
    joint *decisions* are to be made *as far as continuation of the
    counselling is concerned.*

Figure 8.2: Checklist for briefing external advisers or counsellors

These are the most important points that can prevent problems in
the start-up phase of a counselling process. Going through this
checklist creates clarity and openness, and this in itself is a welcome
element in a conflict situation. Agreeing on these points is an
important prerequisite for constructively tackling the conflict,
reducing the danger of 'conflict about the conflict resolution'.

The following points will help conflict parties to orientate
themselves and increase the chances of success for external

counselling. To do this, I will highlight some methods that might be used by external advisers. However, there are no standardized or universally recognized methods, and the adviser or counsellor may proceed in a completely different way. The quality of external advice is therefore not determined by the application of one of the methods mentioned here but by whether you – as somebody who is involved in the conflict – understand how the method used is aimed at the core of the conflict mechanisms of the current level.

8.3 At escalation level 5: loss of face

After the dramatic transition to the fifth level of escalation, the following features will be clearly apparent:

- Moral integrity is lost as a result of public and direct personal attacks.
- 'Unmasking activities' are deliberately staged as a public ritual.
- The exposed 'criminal' is dramatically expelled and 'banished'.
- The exposure causes the 'expellers' to feel dis-illusioned: they see themselves as victims of deception.
- Exposure means that, in retrospect, only the reprehensible aspects of the actions of the exposed 'criminals' are perceived.
- Self-image and enemy image become exaggerated and distorted images of 'angels' as opposed to 'devils', and the negative 'Doubles' dominate events from now on.
- A feeling of physical disgust arises in relation to the expelled person or group.
- The expelled people lose their external perception; they are isolated in the 'echo cave'.
- Contentious issues become fundamental questions about religion, ideology and basic values.
- The expelled people seek rehabilitation at any price.

Figure 8.3: Main characteristics of escalation level 5

External consultancy here has the options of 'process consultation or process counselling' or even 'socio-therapeutic process consultation' (see Figure 6.5). Process consultation deals with people at a deeper level than moderation and supervision and, as a process, takes considerable time. This is because it makes people aware of entrenched patterns of behaviour and attitudes and dissolves them. And in most cases it will also involve a thorough review of all the basic elements of the organization.[2]

'Therapeutic' in this sense does not mean therapy for an individual suffering an illness; rather it denotes forms of dealing with conflict where *pathological patterns in interpersonal relationships* are recognized and treated. This is because of the fact that, although people might exhibit pathological patterns of behaviour towards each other in a conflict situation, the same people will behave completely normally in other situations with other people. Socio-therapeutic process consultation or process counselling is more time-consuming than simple process consultation because it has to deal with deeply rooted suspicions, with fears and deep wounds. A more in-depth approach is required to deal with shattered trust and damaged self-esteem.

As a party in a conflict you can do a lot to support external professional advisers in their work. Even at this stage you will still be able to do a lot yourself. A particularly helpful method is the technique of 'golden moments' (Figure 3.7), because it sharpens people's perception of the tiniest positive aspects of their opponent, helping the conflict parties to find positive triggers for subsequent steps.

At this level external advisers can still use methods already described for the self-help stage in Chapter 7:

- role-negotiation (Figure 7.11 and 7.12)
- clarifying self-image and image of the other (Figure 7.15)
- micro-analysis of critical episodes (Figure 7.17 and 7.18)
- dissolving unwritten role contracts (Figure 7.19).

But working with these methods at level 5 without the help of a third party holds too great a risk of entanglement. The mediator or adviser will check whether discussions in the course of these exercises exhibit the mechanisms of this level of conflict. If this is the case the conflict parties – 'caught red-handed' – can recognize the conflict mechanisms and their consequences and can consciously take counter-measures.

As conflict parties you will endanger the process of resolving the conflict if, as a result of your experience so far, you suspiciously shut yourself off against the opposing party's attempts to open up.

8.4 At escalation level 6: strategies of threat

Once direct attacks have taken place, the disagreement becomes much more radical and violent. Remember the main features:

- The spiral of threats and counter-threats accelerates.
- The triangle of threats comes in and works through a correlation of:
  1. Demand = 2. Punishment = 3. Punishment potential = credibility through proportionality
- The fighting parties lock in themselves and each other ('trip wires') in order to show how determined they are.
- With each threat the conflict parties create for themselves a compulsion to act.
- The 'threateners' lose initiative.
- Stress is continuously increased through ultimatums of demands and counter-demands.
- 'Scissor effects' arise continuously: increasingly important decisions have to be made in a shortening space of time; fewer actions mean that the consequences become increasingly complex.
- A speeding-up is experienced everywhere; events come thick and fast; the mood is increasingly hectic and panicky.

Figure 8.4: Main characteristics of escalation level 6

External consultancy can be successful when the interlocking of the conflict parties – which has led to a series of 'short circuit' actions – can be loosened or broken. This is because, as conflict parties, your actions are increasingly other-directed, i.e. they are reactive rather than active! Using the following methods (Figure 8.5 and 8.6), the external third party can try to soften or dissolve the mutual conditioning. Initially you can carry out the exercise on your own – separately from the opposing party. External people can be very helpful in this.

Select a typical episode in which you felt largely 'imprisoned by the enemy', i.e. where you reacted compulsively, without freedom:

1. Describe the key events in this situation (and perhaps two further situations); be specific and give details: 'When Anthony did this ... and said "..." I had no choice but to do ...'
2. Carefully examine Anthony's 'imprisoning' behaviour and describe the aspects of his behaviour that affected you like a 'red rag'.
3. Articulate how you feel in situations such as these – it's best to use 'I-messages' (see Figure 6.3).
4. Now describe the reactions this provoked or triggered in you; demonstrate as specifically as possible what you do in these situations.
5. What annoys you about your own reactions? What would you have liked to avoid in the situation? What can you not manage to do?
6. Can you think of alternative ways of behaviour in this situation? Collect alternatives and try out a few. Ask for feed-back on how these affect other people.
7. So far you have only considered where Anthony's behaviour triggered weaknesses and unsatisfactory reactions in you; now check where your own behaviour might have had similar effects in provoking Anthony. Collect your ways of behaviour, act them out in an exaggerated form by accompanying them with as much noise as possible.

8. Remember the exaggerated behaviour and accompanying noises, and periodically look back on your own behaviour towards other people in tense situations.

Figure 8.5: Freeing up the interlocking by 'de-conditioning' [3]

The effect of this exercise can be further increased if you exaggerate your own behaviour still further in Steps 4 and 5. You can go as far as being ridiculous. In his work as a psychotherapist Viktor Frankl[4] developed a method which helps timid people to exaggerate their own aberrant behaviour – of which they are frightened – in such a way that it appears ludicrous to themselves. Once this person starts to laugh, they have made the first step in getting out of the stranglehold of their fear. Later, in situations which trigger their fear, this will help them to remember spontaneously the exaggeration of their own behaviour. As soon as they do this, the provocative behaviour of the opposing party will lose its compulsive effect, at least for a short time. But this will be enough to avoid falling into rash short circuit actions and instead to stop and think before responding to the opponent and to think of another way of behaving. In real situations this is unlikely to work first time, but success will come with practice.

The next method (Figure 8.6) can also be useful for external consultancy, in that it gradually begins to reduce the existing tensions by means of unilateral concessions. One thing is important: by making a concession, you don't make yourself dependent on the opposing party – you regain self-control instead.

The aim of the GRIT method (Graduated and Reciprocated Initiatives in Tension-reduction) is to liberate the parties from their interdependence. One conflict party's autonomy to act is strengthened through unilateral concessions to reduce the tension, because it does not make its actions dependent on the behaviour of the opposing party.

1. Think of three tension-reducing initiatives – A, B and C – which might be implemented gradually. The effect of your

initiatives should gradually become greater, so that this can be experienced as an increase. You must be able to implement all the initiatives on your own. These can be small steps, but they must be significant enough to be noticed and taken seriously by the opposing party. External advisers will help you to critically review the implications of the initiatives.

2. Announce Initiative A so that it is specific and clear, giving a date for implementation and attracting the other side's attention. And invite the opposing party to undertake a similar initiative.
3. Implement Initiative A. If the opposing party responds with hostility, protest publicly and clearly, but carry out your initiative as planned and announced.
4. Announce Initiative B and invite the opposing party to undertake an initiative in the same spirit.
5. Implement Initiative B – and protest against unfriendly or hostile actions by your opponent. But do not allow them to stop you from properly implementing the initiative.
6. Announce Initiative C and again invite the opposing party to reciprocate with a friendly action, etc.

Figure 8.6: Unilateral concessions for gradually reducing tensions, after the GRIT method[5]

The GRIT method has often been used successfully as a way of creating trust. Using this technique, former Soviet President Mikhail Gorbachev achieved a decisive breakthrough in international disarmament negotiations!

However, one thing is vital when preparing and announcing the first step: you must always be prepared for disappointing responses from your opponent! Once the conflict has escalated as far as this level, any unilateral good-will action is likely to be met with suspicion. After all, it might just be propaganda, or even a trap. Prepare for how you want to behave if you are met with lack of understanding or even with malicious rejection. You should only announce Initiative A when you are sure that you will remain firm even if you meet with rejection or scorn. And you must be prepared to forgive many times.

Perhaps such concessions and other activities in the process of external counselling might even bring about a turn of events.

8.5 At escalation level 7: limited destructive blows

If the threats don't achieve the desired effect, the parties resort to limited destructive blows. This level is characterized by the following features:

- The parties' thinking only revolves around 'inanimate objects'.
- Human qualities are no longer considered in decisions and action.
- Limited destruction is seen as an 'appropriate response'; counterblows that are out of proportion are still avoided.
- Values and virtues are turned into their opposites: relatively small damage caused to the opposing side is considered a 'benefit' for one's own side.

Figure 8.7: Main characteristics of escalation level 7

Mediation in the classic sense is required on this level, if not before. A mediator will use negotiation techniques in order to bring the conflict parties closer together. Suggestions are offered in the course of 'shuttle diplomacy' and their acceptability is checked. This book is not intended to deal in detail with negotiation techniques, but Fisher/Brown (1989), Fisher/Ury/Patton (1995) and particularly Carlisle/Parker (1989) are close to my own approach and offer help with preparing for negotiation.

Mediation techniques deliberately do not delve deeply.[6] Classic mediation does not seek to heal pathological patterns of behaviour or attitudes but concentrates instead on factual agreements between the conflict parties. Mediation doesn't work directly on the deep mistrust and vengeful thinking that blocks potential solutions. It is well known that the blockages which can cause mediation to fail stem particularly from the area of people's emotions and will.

From this escalation level onwards a conflict party must be prepared for self-confrontation. It must consider carefully what might actually be achieved by continuing the conflict, and what might be the price of further escalation. Challenging by external mediators can help to critically check the situation in which the party makes its decisions:

- What do you risk by continuing the fight?
- What is in danger if you bring about an end to the conflict?
- How can you check whether your assessment of the chances of winning and losing is realistic?
- Where might your own blind spots be?
- What stops you from merely opting out of the conflict?

As this level of escalation marks the beginning of the slow but inevitable descent into the abyss, retreat or leaving the arena without a fight is always more sensible than doggedly continuing the conflict.

8.6 At escalation level 8: fragmentation of the enemy

On crossing the threshold to level 8, the parties give up any willingness to limit the violence used and the damage inflicted. As a reminder, here are the most important features of this level:

- Each party wants to bring about the breakdown of the enemy system.
- They try to destroy vital system factors or key parts and thus make the system unmanageable.
- The fighting parties do everything they can to isolate the opposing party's 'front fighters' from their 'hinterland'.
- The aim is complete destruction of the enemy: body, soul and spirit.

Figure 8.8: Main characteristics of escalation level 8

Mediation can prove difficult even at level 7 when the conflict parties are no longer able to make any contributions of their own to solve the conflict. Mediators may be able to get the parties to agree to voluntary arbitration on the most important contentious issues. Often this becomes possible as a result of great pressure from outside, as individuals or bodies around the conflict parties are interested in limiting the damage.

Voluntary arbitration is only possible if the opposing parties can at least agree on a few key points and document these in a 'declaration of submission' (Figure 8.9).

We (the parties),
through our authorized representatives (names, function), declare that we are prepared to submit to arbitration under the following conditions:

1. The *contentious issues* are described as follows: '...'
    Generally the following are defined precisely:
    a) What are the disputed facts? What exactly is the question?
    b) Which norm, agreement or rules might be violated through this?

2. The *following people* form the arbitration tribunal: '...'

3. The arbitration tribunal assures strictest impartiality and correctness and proceeds according to the following *rules:*

4. The members of the arbitration tribunal are granted *free access* to the organization and *unrestricted access* to documents, files and records belonging to the conflict parties.

5. The arbitration tribunal can, if this is required to carry out their brief swiftly, make a *binding interpretation* of the contentious norms, agreements or rules according to the principles of the governing law.

6. The arbitration tribunal will draw up its *standing orders* and communicate these to the parties to the contract.

7. The final decision of the arbitration tribunal will be recognized in the same way as a court judgement and can be *executed.*

*Figure 8.9: Key points in a declaration of submission
for an arbitration contract*

Agreeing on the composition of an arbitration tribunal can be difficult. It has proved beneficial if each conflict party appoints one person who has its trust to become a member of the tribunal. If this results in an even number of members, the tribunal members themselves appoint an additional person as chair.

Arbitration only makes sense for limited contentious issues which can be decided on by external parties. Many disputed points – if not most! – cannot be resolved in this way. But the arbitration decision can prepare the ground for further mediation if the damage limitation achieved in joint discussion has restored a minimum of trust that can encourage the parties to continue seeking a solution.

8.7 At escalation level 9: together into the abyss

If destruction of the enemy only appears possible through self-destruction, one of the conflict parties may not even stop at its own downfall. The features of the final level are as follows:

- The parties see no acceptable way back: 'We have to move forward at any cost – there is no going back!'
- The conflict parties go for total confrontation.
- Complete destruction of the enemy is the sole aim, even at the price of self-destruction.
- The parties experience a sense of enjoyment in self-destruction: The main thing is that the enemy is ruined!
- They are willing to cause severe damage to the environment or successors through their own downfall.

Figure 8.10: Main characteristics of escalation level 9

This is where the path of destruction and self-destruction reaches its fatal end, unless a last-minute turnaround can be brought about. Even at this threshold it is still possible to stop and think. The parties don't have to jump into the abyss, taking the hated enemy with them. I still think it is more honourable to opt out of the vicious circle of destruction than stubbornly and unscrupulously clinging to a goal and even deriving enjoyment from one's own downfall.

If disaster is to be prevented, it may be possible to mobilize a 'superior power', one with more authority and/or influence. Perhaps this superior power might be able to halt the disaster – usually by applying force. But there is always a danger that the conflict will escalate even faster and further.

A totally different way out of the conflict is to renounce violence completely, as practised in the 'non-violent' approaches of Gandhi, Martin Luther King and others. It may be that outsiders intervene between the parties, completely without violence and with great courage, to try to stop the insanity of destruction.

Which way I go in this extreme situation depends on whether – even in the darkest moments of my life – I am still able to open up to my Higher Self. Of course, this could and should happen in earlier stages of conflict escalation – but it is never too late for the miracle of finding oneself.

9. Self-knowledge and self-help in conflicts

Throughout this book I wanted to encourage you to approach existing and future interpersonal conflicts with confidence and inner strength.

It also helps to distinguish between *differences* and *social conflicts*. In conflict situations it is not the existence of differences that is problematic, but the way in which they are handled.

The two extreme attitudes of *conflict avoidance* (escape) and *belligerence* (aggression) do not allow a constructive and creative resolution of differences or conflicts. Consistent practice can, however, contribute to overcome conflict avoidance and belligerence through an attitude of *assertiveness* and *considerate confrontation*. This is because *assertiveness* combines the positive aspects of the two extreme attitudes and brings them into appropriate alignment.

Assertiveness is the basis of *personal conflict capability*. This means that you are able to do three things:
- perceive and understand conflict symptoms
- be firm and truthful and
- increasingly align your will and your practical abilities.

Perceptiveness, good judgement and ability to act are the main elements of personal conflict capability, which can only be acquired through persistent practice.

A further requirement is an insight into the personal factors of *perceptions, ideas and thinking, as well as feeling, will and actions* which are subject to severe deformation and impairment in conflict situations. Through *self-infection* mechanisms a situation arises in which you don't have a conflict but the conflict has you. Thus you reach the *limits of self-help*. Once you are in this stage, you are well-advised to enlist *collegial help* or *external professional advice*.

However, as a conflict party you can do a lot before things get this far, provided you work on your own personality. This is because people are the most important 'tool' for resolving conflict! This is why dealing with your own *Light and Shadow* is an important prerequisite for an open encounter with your opponent. The same goes for external professional advisers. In every conflict situation professional advisers work on, they are confronted with their own Light and Shadow in the same way as the conflict parties themselves.

Through a good knowledge of the *mechanisms of escalation* you can understand and influence events. The more accurately you are able to assess the *levels of conflict,* the better you will be able to recognize the *possibilities and limits of self-help* and to utilize the opportunities that exist.

Many methods can help you to *signal the existence of conflicts* and to work on the typical problems of the first levels of escalation. I have presented *aids to orientation* for the later levels, which enable you to understand the approaches professional advisers and mediators might take. A checklist of *important points for briefing external advisers* is intended to help the conflict parties when commissioning help, and to aid in ending the conflict about the conflict resolution. This is the only way to limit the damage and to reap benefit from the differences that were recognized.

In many organizations paradoxical things happen:
- Conflicts often result from diffuse or contradictory aims, inhuman structures, unclear job descriptions, badly devised processes or unsuitable resources and tools. Although these problems are rooted in the *organization,* they become *personified* and individuals are blamed for causing them!
- On the other hand people have become adept at *offloading their personal shortcomings onto the organization* as a consequence of faulty structures, so that they do not have to take on personal responsibility.

As a result of this mutual blaming and offloading, causes and solutions are continually sought in the wrong place. This is the best way to maintain existing unresolved conflicts in an organization!

However, a constructive way towards a solution is to see the *interdependence* of the human and organizational aspects of the conflicts and to tackle them accordingly. This allows people to gain self-knowledge as a result of conflicts. If they accept responsibility for their contribution to the conflict, they will come face-to-face with their limits and weaknesses. And painful encounters will give them impulses for personal development. Without conflict, they probably wouldn't have taken these impulses as seriously. This is because conflicts challenge people to assume existential positions – nobody can remain lukewarm or disinterested. Escaping doesn't work either: nobody can run away from themselves.

If people are able to recognize signals of conflict and if organizations creatively tackle signals of differences and tensions, then conflict can enable development. Old habits and structures are shattered and overcome, and new forms are worked out in committed discussions. This goes for individuals as well as for groups.

Nowadays developing conflict capability is one of the most important requirements for a group which embarks on a journey into the social unknown. This goes for groups who set out to realize new things in their work – for example in the areas of complementary medicine, ecological building methods, organic farming or pupil-centred teaching – and it also applies in situations where people seek to try out new forms of co-operation, leadership and organization. In these situations it is vital to improve personal conflict capability. Even if a group subscribes to new values, ideals and concepts, old ways of thinking persist in their words and actions far longer than they themselves notice.

One thing is probably clear: you can't practise conflict capability in social isolation. Learning and practising is only possible *in and through the group.* When co-operation turns to competitiveness and tensions escalate, conflicts always point to your greatest developmental challenges. You should ask yourself: where did I meet limits? Which capabilities are required from me in the conflict situation? Where can the conflict help me to develop? What can we learn as a group by accepting the challenge of the conflict? This is because a group, in working together, always embarks on a joint developmental journey, even if it is unaware of this.

If conflict capability is not practised, courage becomes rashness, caution becomes cowardice. Trying out completely new social forms demands that all the people involved discard old habits, both personally and in the group, and that they try out new, largely unprecedented skills. This is what distinguishes *progression* from *regression* (Figure 9.1).

	Solution/answer:	
Challenge/question:	... old, proven answer	... new, previously unknown answer
old question and ...	conservatism routine	innovation creativity
new question and ...	stagnation or even regression	progress

Figure 9.1: Opportunities and risks – progression and regression

If *new* questions arise for the group, but the group answers these questions by resorting to *old* solutions, which may have been successful in the past, there may be a temporary or permanent recourse to outdated developmental stages: this is *regression*. However, if a group is prepared to seek new answers to new questions, then this can lead to innovation. People look for new values, ideas and concepts and try them out on a joint learning journey. This is a change in the basic ideas, a change of the 'paradigms', leading to progress and development.

This developmental journey does, of course, involve continuous searching and experimenting, discovery and making mistakes.

Sometimes it is possible to break new ground, on other occasions there are throwbacks to the old ways. But individuals and groups experience the tension between the old and the new on a daily basis. Therefore the path of innovation is always stony and paved with conflict. Some things may have appeared new at first glance but on closer examination turned out to be a rehash of the old.

So conflicts and crises have *two sides:* they are *dangers and opportunities* at the same time. Therefore conflicts always hold the risk that people will cling to old habits even more. They drift down the path of *regression* that leads through the various levels of escalation into the depths of human sub-nature. But conflicts also provide the opportunity to embark on a journey of *progress* and to break new ground.

As a human being I can allow counter-forces to affect my actions even by being just slightly careless. If my perception is increasingly impaired (as described in Chapter 1), I won't notice that my thoughts, feelings, will and actions are less and less self-directed and increasingly other-directed. I react instead of acting and provoke rash responses to my actions and omissions in the opposing party. I act less and less from my Light but allow myself to be driven by my Shadow. My consciousness is gradually weakened. This leads to the development of the inherent dynamics of escalation, which drives the conflict downwards. But this doesn't just happen to me 'by fate': I can recognize that it is happening at any time, and that I can end or change it.

Whether I can muster sufficient staying power and assertiveness against the propelling and suction force of conflict dynamics depends on whether I can connect with my Higher Self.

The concepts and techniques described in this book are intended to offer help to find oneself, and thus to find the true being of the other person. They are intended to help awaken awareness and morality.

When this succeeds, I have my fate in my own hands. I decide whether the conflict leads downwards or upwards.

Chapter notes

Chapter 1. Help – Conflict!
1   Cf Glasl 1992
2   Rather than using both masculine and feminine forms each time, I will alternate from chapter to chapter
3   Cf Richter 1980
4   Thomas 1976, Smith 1981
5   Cf Schwarz 1995
6   After Peter Block 1986
7   Glasl
8   Glasl
9   Glasl 1997
10 Glasl 1997
11 Glasl 1997
12 For an in-depth analysis, see Glasl 1997, pp. 34-46
13 Glasl 1997, pp. 148f

Chapter 2. Personality as a source of social conflict
1   Glasl 1997, p. 25ff
2   Cf Lievegoed 1997
3   Frankl 1969, p. 76
4   Müller-Wiedemann 1980
5   Lievegoed 1997, Treichler 1989
6   Jung GW 7
7   Lievegoed 1997
8   1973, pp. 16ff
9   Maslow 1968
10 Richter 1967, 1972
11 ibid
12 Allport 1954, Lückert 1957, Rochblave-Spenlé 1973
13 Allport 1954, Murray 1933
14 Adorno 1950, Bass/Duntemann 1963, Sherif 1962
15 Eckhardt 1965, White 1966, , Boesch/Earl Davis/Kelman 1964

16 Allport 1954, Glasl 1969
17 Richter, 1967, 1972
18 Steiner (1924) 1996
19 1967, 1972
20 Neuberger 1994
21 Gladstone 1959, Bronfenbrenner 1961, Daim 1962, Smith/ Bruner/White 1964
22 Cf Glasl/Lievegoed 1993
23 Steiner (1924) 1996
24 ibid

Chapter 3. How can I work on myself in conflict situations?

1 After Steiner (1905) 1994
2 After Steiner (1909) 1983
3 Steiner: (1909 and 1910a) 1983
4 ibid, from the chapter, 'The Mission of Anger'
5 Glasl 1997, p. 378
6 Glasl 1997, p. 298f
7 After Block, 1986
8 Hasper/Glasl 1988, p. 74f
9 Steiner (1924) 1996

Chapter 4. How conflicts are driven

1 Filley, 1975, pp. 104ff
2 Richardson 1960

Chapter 5. How conflicts can go downhill

1 Cf Glasl 1997, pp. 183ff, for details
2 Gelner 1967, Rother 1976
3 Berne 1964, Choy 1990, Karpman 1968, Stewart/Jones 1990, Woolams/Brown 1978, Zalcman 1990
4 Argyle 1992
5 Janis 1972
6 Sherif 1962, Gladstone 1959
7 Watzlawick/Beavin/Jackson 1968
8 Lievegoed 1997, 1985
9 Goffman 1955, Garfinkel 1974

10 Fromm 1975
11 Newcomb 1947
12 Goffman 1955
13 Schelling 1960

Chapter 6. What can I do as soon as I notice a conflict?
1   Cf Gordon 1970; Faller/Kerntke/Wackmann 1996 pp. 87/88
2   After Gordon 1970
3   Cf Glasl 1997, pp. 314f
4   Steiner (1921, p. 14)
5   Glasl 1997, pp. 307f

Chapter 7. What can I do myself at the different levels of escalation?
1   Glasl 1997
2   Like a muscle spasm in the body
3   Glasl 1997
4   After Eiseman 1978
5   After NPI (Lievegoed 1974)
6   After Miles 1959, pp. 116f
7   Cf Glasl 1997, pp. 227ff
8   After Eiseman 1978
9   Glasl 1997
10 After Miles 1959
11 After Harrison 1971
12 Adapted from Harrison 1971
13 Steiner (1914) 1991
14 After Blake/Shepard/Mouton 1964
15 Glasl 1997, pp. 331f
16 Glasl 1997
17 Cf Glasl 1997, pp. 330ff
18 Glasl 1997, p. 68
19 Glasl 1997 (English translation): *The Enterprise of the Future*

Chapter 8. Professional help can go further!

1 Glasl 1997
2 Cf Glasl/Lievegoed 1993
3 Glasl 1997, pp. 334f, 378
4 Frankl 1975
5 Osgood 1966
6 Cf Besemer 1995; Folberg/Taylor 1984; Folger/Jones 1994

Bibliography

Adorno, T. W. (1950): *The Authoritarian Personality.* New York
Allport, G. W. (1954): *The Nature of Prejudice.* Double Anchor
Argyle, M. (1992): *Bodily Communication.* London
Bach, G. R./Deutsch R .M. (1980): *Halt! Mach mich nicht verrückt.*
    Düsseldorf/Cologne
Bach, G. R./ Wyden P, (1983): *Streiten verbindet.* Frankfurt.
Bass, B. M./Dunteman J. (1963): 'Biases in the evaluation of one's own
    group, its allies and opponents' in: *Journal of Conflict Resolution,*
    vol. 7/1963, pp. 16-20
Berne, E. (1964): *Games People Play.* New York
Besemer, C. (1995): *Mediation. Vermittlung in Konflikten.* Baden
Bittlestone, A. (1980): *Our Spiritual Companions. From Angels and
    Archangels to Cherubim and Seraphim.* Edinburgh
Blake, R./Shepard H./Mouton J. (1964): *Managing Intergroup
    Conflict in Industry.* Ann Arbor/Houston
Block, P. (1986): *Workshop 'Designed Learning'.* Plainfield (New Jersey)
Boesch, E. E./Davis Earl E./Kelman H. C. (1964): *Vorurteile, ihre
    Erforschung und ihre Bekämpfung.* Frankfurt
Bronfenbrenner, U. (1961): 'The "Mirror Image" of Soviet-American
    Relations' in: *Journal of Social Issues,* vol. 17/1961, pp. 45-56
Bush, R./Folger J. (1994): *The Promise of Mediation.* San Francisco
Carlisle, J./Parker R. C. (1989): *Beyond Negotiation.* Chichester/
    New York
Choy, A. (1990): 'The Winner's Triangle' in: *Transactional Analysis
    Journal* (TAJ), 1/1990
Daim, W. (1962): 'Das Bild des Feindes' in: *Der Christ in der Welt.*
    Vienna, Nr. 4/1962, pp. 124-132
Eckhardt, W. (1965): 'War Propaganda, Welfare Values, and Political
    Ideologies' in: *Journal of Conflict Resolution,* vol. 9/1965, pp. 345-358
Eiseman, J. W. (1978): 'Reconciling "Incompatible Positions"' in:
    Journal of Applied Behavioral Science, vol. 14,1978, pp. 133-150
Faller, K./Kerntke W./Wackmann M.(1996): *Konflikte selber lösen.*
    Mühlheim an der Ruhr

Filley, A. C. (1975): *Interpersonal Conflict Resolution*. Dallas/Oakland

Fine, N./Macbeth F.(1992): *Playing with fire. Training for the Creative Use of Conflict*. Leicester/London

Fisher, R./Brown S. (1989): *Gute Beziehungen. Die Kunst der Konfliktvermeidung, Konfliktlösung und Kooperation*. Munich

Fisher, R./Ury W./Patton B. (1991): *Getting to Yes: negotiating agreement without giving in*. Houghton Mifflin

Folberg, J./Taylor A. (1984): *Mediation. A Comprehensive Guide to Resolving Conflicts without Ligitation*. San Francisco

Folger, J./Jones T. (eds.) (1994): *New Directions in Mediation*. Thousand Oaks/London/New Delhi

Frankl, V. E. (1969): 'Der Wille zum Sinn und seine Frustration durch die moderne Industriegesellschaft' in: Gottlieb Duttweiler-Institut (ed.): *Hemmende Strukturen in der heutigen Industriegesellschaft*. Zürich 1969

Frankl, V. E. (1975): *Theorie und Therapie der Neurosen*. Munich/Basel

Fromm, E. (1975): *The Anatomy of Human Destructiveness*. Connecticut

Garfinkel, H. (1974): 'Bedingungen für den Erfolg von Degradierungszeremonien' in: *Gruppendynamik* magazine, April 1974 (Richardson 1960)

Gelner, C. (1967): *Die Kunst des Verhandelns*. Heidelberg

Gladstone, A. (1959): 'The Conception of the Enemy' in: *Journal of Conflict Resolution*, vol. 3/1959, pp. 132-137

Glasl, F. (1969): 'Techniken der Konfliktlösung' in: *Der Christ in der Welt*. Vienna, Sept. 1969

Glasl, F. (1982): 'The Process of Conflict Escalation and Roles of Third Parties' in Bomers G./R. Peterson (eds.): *Conflict Management and Industrial Relations*. Boston/The Hague/London

Glasl, F. (1992): 'Die grossen Konflikte der Gegenwart und ihre Auswirkungen auf die Unternehmen' in: Demuth, A. (ed.): *Konfliktmanagement und Umweltstrategien*. Imageprofile '92. Düsseldorf/Vienna/New York/Moscow

Glasl, F. (trans.1997): *The Enterprise of the Future*. Stroud

Glasl, F. (1997): *Konfliktmanagement. Ein Handbuch für Führungskräfte, Beraterinnen und Berater*. Bern/Stuttgart

Glasl, F. (1997a): 'Der Weg in die Zukunft ist mit Konflikten gepflastert' in: J.-C. Lin/Neider A. (ed.): *Almanach 1997 "Der Weg in die Zukunft"*. Stuttgart

Glasl, F. (1998): *Konfliktfähigkeit statt Streitlust.* Dornach
Glasl, F./Brugger E. (ed.) (1994): *Der Erfolgskurs Schlanker Unternehmen. Impulstexte und Praxisbeispiele.* Bern/Wien
Glasl, F./Lievegoed B.(1993): *Dynamische Unternehmensentwicklung.* Bern/Stuttgart 1993
Gleich, S. von (1975): *Die Umwandlung des Bösen.* Basel
Goffman, B. (1955): 'On Face-Work' in: *Psychiatry,* vol. 18, 1955, pp. 211-231
Gordon, T. (1970): *Parent Effectiveness Training.* Wyden, New York
Gordon, T. (1974): *Teacher Effectiveness Training.* Wyden, New York
Harrison, R. (1971): 'Role Negotiation: a tough-minded approach to team development' in: Burke W./Hornstein H.: *The Social Technology of Organization Development.* Washington 1971
Hasper, W./Glasl F. (1988): *Von kooperativer Marktstrategie zur Unternehmensentwicklung.* Bern/Stuttgart
Janis, I. L. (1972): *Victims of Groupthink.* Atlanta etc.
Jordan, T. (1997): 'Achtsamkeit im Umgang mit Konflikten' in: *Transpersonale Psychologie und Psychotherapie.* 1/1997, pp. 78-101
Julich, H. (1954): *In Gegensätzen miteinander. Ein Grundproblem anthroposophischer Gesellschaftsbildung.* Freiburg im Breisgau
Jung, C. G. (GW 7a 1992): *Psychology of the Unconscious.* London
Jung, C. G. (GW 7b 1953): *The Relations Between the Ego and the Unconscious.* London
Jung, C. G. (1990): *Man and his Symbols.* London
Karpman, S. (1968): 'Fairy Tale and Script Drama Analysis' in: *Transaktionsanalyse-Bulletin* 7/1968
Klünker, W. U. (1988): *Johannes Scotus Erigena, Denken im Gespräch mit dem Engel.* Stuttgart
Leymann, H./Niedl K. (1994): *Mobbing. Psychoterror am Arbeitsplatz.* Vienna
Lievegoed, B. (1973): *The Developing Organisation.* Tavistock, London
Lievegoed, B. (1997): *Phases: the Spiritual Rhythms of Adult Life.* Sophia Books
Lievegoed, B. (1985): *Man on the Threshold.* Stroud
Lückert, H.-R. (1957): *Konflikt-Psychologie. Einführung und Grundlegung.* Munich/Basel
Lüdemann-Ravit, P. (1994): *Konflikt-Sprechstunde.* Stuttgart

Mahringer, E./Steinweg R. (1997): *Konstruktive Haltungen und Verhaltensweisen.* Berlin

Martens, G. (1990): *Auch Eltern waren Kinder. Ursachen und Lösungen von Konflikten in der Familie.* Munich

Maslow, A. H. (1968): *Towards a Psychology of Being.* New York

Miles, M. B. (1959): *Learning to Work with Groups.* New York

Müller-Wiedemann, H. (1980): *Mitte der Kindheit.* Stuttgart

Murray, H. A. (1933): 'The Effect of Fear upon Estimates of Maliciousness of the Other Personalities' in: *Journal of Social Psychology,* vol. 4/1933, pp. 310-329

Neuberger, O. (1994): *Mobbing. Übel mitspielen in Organisationen.* Munich/Mering

Neuberger, O. (1995): Mikropolitik. *Der alltägliche Aufbau und Einsatz von Macht in Organisationen.* Stuttgart

Newcomb, T. R. (1947): 'Autistic Hostility and Social Reality' in: *Human Relations,* vol. 1, 1947, pp. 69-86

Osgood, C. B. (1966): *Perspective in Foreign Policy.* Palo Alto (Calif.)

Prokofieff, S. (1995): *Rudolf Steiner's Research into Karma and the Mission of the Anthroposophical Society.* London/Temple Lodge

Prokofieff, S. (1995): *The Occult Significance of Forgiveness.* London/Temple Lodge

Redlich, A. (1997): *Konfliktmoderation.* Hamburg

Richardson, L. F. (1960): *Arms and Insecurity.* Pittsburgh

Richter, H.-E. (1967): *Eltern, Kind und Neurose.* Reinbek bei Hamburg

Richter, H.-E. (1972): *Patient Familie.* Reinbek bei Hamburg

Richter, H.-E. (1980): *Flüchten oder Standhalten.* Reinbek bei Hamburg

Rochblave-Spenlé, A.-M. (1973): *Psychologie des Konflikts.* Freiburg

Rother, W. (1967): *Die Kunst des Streitens.* Munich

Rubin, J./Pruitt D./ Kim, S. (1994): *Social Conflict: Escalation, Stalemate and Settlement.* New York

Satir, V. (1978): *Selfworth and Communication.* Munich

Schelling, Th. C. (1960): *Arms and Influence.* New Haven/London

Schroeder, H.-W. (1979): *Mensch und Engel, die Wirklichkeit der Hierarchien.* Stuttgart

Schulz von Thun, F. (1981): *Miteinander reden: Störungen und Klärungen.* Reinbek bei Hamburg